RICHARD ARMSTRONG

Themselves Alone

Houghton Mifflin Company Boston 1972

For Bruce, Pat, Geoff and Talia
with love.

LIBRARY OF CONGRESS CATALOG CARD NUMBER: 76-184248
PRINTED IN THE UNITED STATES OF AMERICA
ISBN: 0-395-13721-7
FIRST PRINTING   C

CONTENTS

To these from birth is Belief forbidden;
From these till death is Relief afar...

Rudyard Kipling
The Sons of Martha, 1907

Introduction

MAN IS A gregarious animal. Ever since he came down out of the trees and walked the earth erect, he has felt the need to form first groups, then tribes, and finally societies. In the beginning this urge was an instinctive response triggered by the need to survive in a hostile environment where he had to compete with other and often larger animals for the available food. But as life on this planet increased in complexity and the struggle for survival became more conscious and therefore more imperative and demanding, so did his getting together with his fellows become more deliberate, more purposeful, and more controlled. In any context, however, control implies rules; and rules, whether they are called laws, ethics, moral obligations, or divine commandments, impose restrictions on those who undertake to observe them. So for man the entry into social relationship with his fellows meant the acceptance of rules, which from the very beginning deprived him of at least some of his freedom. And though each advance made in organization or technology, politics or economics, has increased his expectation of life both in duration and — in some respects — quality, it has also proliferated the rules and regulations and reduced still further his freedoms. Even his ability to think freely is now being steadily eroded by the admen and the media, and to be fully accepted by any society today, he must make himself look, act, and think like every other member of it.

Out of this development, which has a frightening cumulative effect, have come concepts like *the average man, the man in the street, John Citizen,* and *the Consumer* with a capital *C.*

There is, however, no such creature as the average man except in statistics. Gregarious from necessity and to some extent from habit, *homo sapiens* remains, fundamentally and forever, an individual. Otherwise he would still be up in the trees, for it was his difference, his individuality that made the first of his kind come down to live at ground level; and every discovery, every advance made since, however consolidated, was conceived and initiated in the mind and actions of some odd man out, somebody whose individuality was more powerful than the pressures on him to conform.

Such men are the loners — those among us who, for one reason or another and at any cost, must, in the modern idiom, do their own thing. They have always been with us and, if there is to be any future for mankind, we must hope they always will be. Consequently they appear in a variety of roles, not only in written history but also in literature, folklore, and even religion.

The early mariners, pushing beyond the boundaries of a world that had become too small to satisfy their aspirations or perhaps just too sober and rigid to contain their exuberance, were essentially loners; so also were the Pilgrim Fathers, opting out from a society whose values they could no longer subscribe to. Brigham Young, taking off into the blue in 1846 for roughly the same reason, belongs with them; and Christopher Columbus, hawking his bright idea around the courts of Spain and Portugal, was another. One could go on, for such men bob up in the mind like hunks of driftwood in a tiderip, but these few examples will suffice.

Literature is thick with them too, all the way from Apuleius and his *Golden Ass* to Captain Yossarian in *Catch-22*, taking in Shakespeare and Hemingway en route. Robinson Crusoe is perhaps the best known and most minutely observed in isolation; but he was an involuntary loner and there are others that come closer to the heart because their dissent was both conscious and passionately felt. Heathcliff in *Wuthering Heights* wandering the wild moors and matching nature's most savage mood with his own; and Gilliatt in *The Toilers of the Sea* making the ultimate gesture of renunciation at the very moment he attained success.

When we come to folklore, the significant factor in all the stories is not the temporary defeat and eclipse of the hero, but the urge in him to get off alone somewhere and find his true self again in solitude. So Wotan becomes The Wanderer, Alfred the Great meditates while the cakes burn, Robert the Bruce has his encounter with the spider in a cave, and Richard the Lion-Heart makes his pilgrimage with the lute.

It is in the context of religion, however, that the loners are most numerous and come nearest to being understood. Judaism has its Elijah being fed by the ravens; Christianity has John the Baptist and the carpenter's son from Nazareth seeking enlightenment, peace of mind, and their own true selves in the wilderness; and Islam has its *Hegira*. So too with every form of ritualized mysticism right back to the Stone Age — at least some of each generation must leave the comfort and security of the community and walk alone for a while.

In this respect, the loner is not always a folk hero. Society's view of him is two-faced. On the one hand he is the personification of every man's hidden desire to opt out, and on the other he is the scapegoat, the sacrificial victim by whose expulsion the group is purged of its sins and relieved of such evils as sickness and famine. The King of Years in Tibet is an excellent example of this kind of loner. According to James G. Frazer in *The Golden Bough*, he is a man selected from the people, who, after various complicated rituals and ceremonies, goes off into the mountains on a white horse. Provided with the barest necessities for existence, he stays there in complete isolation for a year. The best thing he can do for the community is to die within the period; but if he should survive, he is free to return to Lhasa at the end of it.

The loner's attitude to society, however, is seldom so easy to identify or so simple to define. In modern times, at least, there is usually an avowed and more or less rational reason for his cutting adrift. Like Sir Douglas Mawson seeking the South Magnetic Pole, he is after some geographical discovery; or maybe he is bent on establishing a scientific fact, as Apsley Cherry-Garrard was when he made "the worst journey in the world" to find the egg of an emperor penguin; and the most publicized of our modern loners are out merely to create new records for distance, speed, and/or endurance. The immediate drive is usually less obvious than the ostensible purpose; but in most cases it can be pinpointed with some degree of certainty. Ambition, poverty of a kind, hunger for power, patriotism, vanity, perversity, and an overwhelming craving to prove something to someone, maybe only himself — one, or a combination of any number of these can start a man off into the empty places. But it is from below this again, deep in his heart and instincts, that the real motivation springs.

Geographically the latter-day loner belongs to one or another of four groups: those who have sought their solitude in the desert, those who have striven for the mountaintops, those who have courted torment and flirted with death in the region of the polar ice caps, and those who have pushed their luck to the limit on the oceans of the world.

This listing excludes all the intrepid and often fool-hardy characters who have performed miracles of various kinds in the skies above us. The omission is calculated. There have, of course, been flying men who were true loners. Sir Francis Chichester and Antoine de Saint-Exupéry are two that immediately spring to mind; but as a loner, Sir Francis belongs with the sea and Saint-Ex with the desert. The airman as such is no true loner. The passionate belief that it is better to travel hopefully than to arrive is not for him. Getting there is all-important and he is never alone all that long anyhow. He has his moments, of course. Sir Charles Edward Kingsford-Smith, for instance, recording a pioneer flight across the Pacific in his book *My Flying Life*, begins what could have become a lyrical description of the dawn seen from a great height; but it doesn't gel and long before he can get switched on, he is back with the record he is creating and waving some more flags. His real attitude to empty places is expressed in another passage in the same book. Here he is telling the story of a solo flight from Australia to England in 1931 and complains bitterly about the country in the Middle East, characterizing it as "indescribably dreary, flat and deserted." Flying over it gave him a "sense of utter loneliness"; but even so, his only concern was keeping to his schedule and ahead of his rivals.

To the true loner schedules are anathema and rivalry bunk.

Space is another emptiness left out of the reckoning, for the astronaut is never completely out of touch and never in the strict sense of the word really alone — not while all the systems keep going anyhow. To deny his immense skill or belittle in any way his fantastic courage is the last thing anyone would wish to do; but given all this, he remains more an adjunct to technology — the servant of an enormously complicated machine, the working of which involves hundreds of other men apart from himself — than a man confronting nature alone with nothing but his own two hands and his guts to sustain him. Moreover, he is monitored to the last tiny detail and the ultimate function of his being; and with the backroom boys checking not only his movements and heartbeats, but also the behavior of his digestive tract and the working of his brain, he is less alone than a shoe salesman in a crowd of fifty thousand at a ball game.

Some of the true loners, notably Joshua Slocum and Saint-Exupéry, are wonderfully articulate, and a considerable library could be built up of books by and about them. Nevertheless, a closed mouth would seem to be an essential part of their make-up. Augustine Courtauld, for example. He was a member of the expedition that Gino Watkins led to the Greenland ice cap in the early 1930s. The purpose of the exercise was to study weather conditions along a projected air route. To this end, a dome-tent was set up at a point optimistically called the Central Weather Station, and, on November 15, Courtauld was left there to sit out the sub-Arctic winter on his own. Drifting snow quickly buried him and his instruments in the tent, and there he remained until a relief party found him on May 4 the following year. He was not only alive and well, very dirty and wildly bearded, but also extremely disgruntled at being disturbed. The real point, however, is that his report on the five months and twenty days of utter solitude he had endured ran to only a thousand words — four pages of typescript. Anybody more taciturn than that would be speechless.

The loners in fact are largely a lost legion, and C. T. Madigan's epitaph to the wanderers of the Australian outback would serve for them all. He calls them "the unknown men" and writes:

> Many have passed away, most of them buried in the lonely places where they spent their lives, too poor ever to have retired, too long in the country to face the artificial life of cities at the end. Their dreams never came true, but they always travelled hopefully and now they have arrived. Their graves lie scattered far and wide; little heaps of stone to keep the dingoes away, rough wooden crosses, standing awry, eaten by white ants, drifted over by sand . . .

The contribution of the loners to human progress is immense, yet, with a handful of exceptions, they are indeed unknown to the vast majority of those who, in the last analysis, owe to them everything that remains worthwhile about life on earth. There are memorials of a kind to a few of them — the sea-greened bronze statues to Columbus in the approaches to Huelva and to de Lesseps at the entrance to the Suez Canal; the plaque high up on the side of the Gaillard Cut commemorating the unnamed heroes who dug a way for ships through the Isthmus of Panama; a cairn of stones on Everest; a name here and there on the map of the world — but the rest are unsung. Even the contemporary ones who for one reason or another — usually an image-maker's gimmick — make the headlines, are forgotten as soon as a new sensation crops up.

And the concern here is with loners in the widest possible sense of the term, which includes not only the single-handed sailor and the solitary walker in the wastelands, but others in similar places who strictly speaking were not alone. Besides being different and unpredictable, they were elusive, private men. Pressed to reveal themselves, they would either disappear into the void again or fence themselves around with alibis that concealed both their real motives and their true feelings. The purpose is not to retell their stories as such, but to try and penetrate those alibis to discover what, if anything, they had in common, what moved them, and what was really in it for them.

The place to begin is obviously the desert, since it was there that loners first began wandering in search of themselves.

I

Wanderers in the Wastelands

Desert is the geographer's term for any large tract of barren and uninhabited land. In the widest sense, it includes those frozen areas that fringe the polar regions, both north and south, and terrain such as the Mongolian steppes, which are clothed with vegetation in the springtime and desolate for the rest of the year. But in the minds of most people, the word refers more precisely to hot and dry places where the temperatures are extreme and evaporation rapid, and a shower of rain comes like a near miracle. This kind of total desolation is found both north and south of the Equator. In the Northern Hemisphere three such areas — the Sahara, Libyan, and Nubian deserts — run into each other and cover virtually the whole of North Africa from the Atlantic Ocean to the Red Sea. Eastward from there lie the deserts of Arabia, Iran, Turkestan, and Gobi. There are also the numerous deserts in North America made familiar by the Hollywood film industry and the magazines. South of the Equator they are fewer and usually less extensive, the most notable being the Kalahari in South Africa and the desert regions in the interior of Australia.

The essential characteristic of a desert is lack of rain and the consequent scarcity of moisture in both the earth itself and the air above it. From this it follows that in such areas vegetation is scanty, though it is seldom totally absent. The plants that do grow — prickly cactus with a glossy outer skin that exudes little or no moisture; varieties of spiky grass called spinifex — survive because they are peculiarly adapted to the conditions.

Deserts are not necessarily sandy. There are areas — notably in the Sahara and the southeastern quarter of Arabia — where sand dunes, stretching to an unbroken circle of horizon like great waves suddenly and forever immobilized, are the predominant feature; but elsewhere there are high plateaus of riven rock, tracts of wind-rounded pebbles, salt pans and, in Australia, vast flat beds of glittering gypsum. The extraordinary variety of desert terrain is vividly described in T. E. Lawrence's account of his epic journey from Wejd on the Red Sea through Arfaja, Bair, and Jefer to Akaba. After leaving the coast, they went, he says:

> . . . up a tributary valley which soon widened into the plain of the Shegg — a sand flat. About it, in scattered confusion, sat small islands and pinnacles of red sandstone, grouped like seracs,

wind-eroded at the bases till they looked very fit to fall and block the road which wound in and out between them, through narrows seeming to give no passage, but always opening into another bay of blind alleys . . .

By sundown on the same day, they had left the sandstone and were on blue-black volcanic rock, which was mainly in the form of worn basalt blocks no bigger than fists, bedded together like a pavement of cobbles over the "hard, black cinder-debris of themselves. . . ." Next day, they were back on the red sandstone again, winding their way among "crazy chimneys from which the harder layers projected knife sharp in level shelves beyond the soft crumbling rock . . ." The day after that they were on flat slatelike slabs as much as ten feet square and four inches thick. Then came sand interrupted by mile-square patches of dried mud called *giaan*, white and polished smooth by the action of the wind on its surface. And so it went on every day of the two-month-long journey, changing in a single stride from sand to rock, rock to pebble, pebble to mud, and mud back to sand again.

Another popular misconception about deserts is that they are all low-lying and flat. Parts of the Arabian desert are 3000 feet above sea level and, leaving aside rock faces and the deep gashes made by the occasional cloudbursts, even the dunes, wind-driven, often pile up into waves over 100 feet high with a drop like a cliff on the leeward side.

Temperatures in these areas are extreme. In the daytime it is not unusual for the air to reach 120 degrees Fahrenheit and the surface underfoot 30 or more degrees higher than that; at night in the same area the thermometer will register temperatures below freezing.

Perhaps the most striking feature common to all deserts is the mirage. This is an atmospheric effect found when there is no wind in areas subject to great heat or cold. It is caused by reflection and refraction of light on atmosphere of different densities lying in layers. In these conditions two images are projected, one of them inverted. Thus, ships below the horizon at sea are sometimes seen upside down above it and, in the desert, remote clouds are reflected on the sand like expanses of water. Stories are told of men being lured to their death by the mirage in the desert, but the experienced, even the merely competent traveler in such regions is hardly likely to be deceived by it.

In spite of the essentially arid nature of these territories, water is found within their boundaries. It has three sources: dug wells, artesian bores, and natural springs. The dug wells are often very deep and there are hand-excavated water holes in the Rub' al Khali going down 17 fathoms (102 feet) and no timber available for shoring.

The shallower dug wells are often brackish, but water from an artesian well is invariably sweet. This particular technological development, now used extensively in the Australian outback, has done as much in its way as the internal combustion engine to conquer the wilderness and cut it down to size. Boreholes are taken down to great depths, over 2000 feet being quite common and 6000 not unknown.

But for wonder and beauty, nothing can beat the natural spring in the desert and the demiparadise that comes into being in the fertile soil around it. This is the oasis. There are many in the deserts of the world; but that encountered by Lawrence at El Kurr is perhaps the essence of them all. It was occupied by an Arab called Dhaif-Allah and his daughters and they had made of it a "green garden in the desert." They grew tobacco, beans, melons, cucumbers, and eggplants with low palms for shade; and, wanting nothing from or for others and only the garden for themselves, they were free.

Apart from the testing physical strains associated with long abstinence from such products of organized society as regular meals, well cooked and adequately presented, hot baths, frequent changes of underwear, comfortable beds, and shelter from the elements, the desert presents a number of positive hazards to those who haunt it.

Quicksands are one thing. These can be of considerable extent and they give little or no warning of the danger they constitute for unwary feet. The area in Arabia known as Um as Samin is a case in point. It looks like any other salt flat except for its enormous size — two days' march in every direction, it is said — but the local Bedouins avoid it and many strangers are supposed to have been swallowed by it. Another such area is recorded at Bahr as Safi in the Hadhramaut. Here the sand is described as an impalpable powder and an experiment with a weight on a six-fathom line saw the bare end disappear in roughly five minutes.

Another peril is the sandstorm — a hot, dust-laden wind sometimes called the *khamsin*, which reduces visibility to zero and quickly blots out both tracks and landmarks, throwing the wayfarer back onto his compass if he has one and immobilizing him if he hasn't. To sit huddled in the lee of a tent, listening to the hiss of the driven sand while struggling for breathable air under a head covering is bad enough, but to ride in the *khamsin* is nothing less than torment. The air is so dry that moving into it, the lips first shrivel, then crack open and where the face is exposed it becomes chapped to rawness. But it is the eyes that suffer most. "Our eyelids," says Lawrence, describing a march in a sandstorm, "gone granular, seemed to creep back and bare our shrinking eyes."

Losing contact with one's transport, whether it is a splayfooted camel, a jeep, or an airplane, is another disaster to be avoided; so is running it into the ground. Yet this is probably the commonest initial cause of desert tragedies. Gibson, one of the earliest in the Australian wilderness, went this way a hundred years ago and he is just one of many, known and unknown, both before and since.

But whatever desert a man wanders, he can suffer no more terrible fate than to run out of water and be unable to replenish his supply within a reasonable time and distance. In these circumstances it isn't an oasis with date palms and watermelons growing around it that he craves, but any kind of stinking water hole; and the distances between them are often enormous. In Australia, for instance, Edward John Eyre, traveling with packhorses, once walked 160 miles between water holes and then had to dig for it; and Harry St. John Philby, in his journey across the empty quarter of Arabia, covered a dry stretch of 375 miles.

The most self-sufficient wanderers in any empty space are, of course, the aborigines of Australia. In certain areas where there is no surface water and the only moisture lies too deep for digging, vegetation of a kind — fine grass and sparse shrubs with odd patches of gum scrub — still survives. Here, in the night, dew collects like spangles on the bushes; and in the brief period between daybreak and sunrise, the aborigine collects these droplets with a handful of grass, using it like a sponge and squeezing it out into a container. Three or four men, working in a team, have been known to collect a quart of water in this way; but they must know exactly when to start and then work fast, for as soon as the sunlight strikes the shrub, the dew-drops fall and are lost in the parched ground beneath it.

Another trick described by Eyre is to find a patch of gum scrub in a hollow, or failing that, on flat ground between two ridges. A likely-looking tree is selected and a trench dug a little way out from the trunk to expose the lateral roots, which are of great length. One root about two inches in diameter is severed from the tree and twenty to thirty feet of its length dug or dragged up out of the ground. This root is then peeled of its bark and broken into small pieces, which have the sap shaken out of them in turn into some kind of receptacle. A good root might yield as much as two thirds of a pint in less than half an hour and make the difference between life and death for the operator.

There is no more terrifying prospect than death by thirst; yet it is not a long process, least of all in hot deserts.

> . . . not a long death [wrote Lawrence]. Even for the very strongest a second day in summer was all — but very painful; for thirst was an active malady; a fear and panic which tore at the brain and reduced the bravest man to a stumbling, babbling maniac in an hour or two; and then the sun killed him.

It is difficult to imagine the degree of dedication or perversity needed to bring a man to the point of chancing such an end; easier, perhaps, to put him down in the record as suffering from some peculiar and completely private form of madness. Too easy!

So now, having looked at deserts in general, the next step is to examine three of them in particular and, of all those who have wandered there, to select a handful who stand out from the rest. It may be that they spring to mind because of their achievements, but they are included here simply because they are the most articulate and therefore most likely to reveal their hidden selves and underlying motives.

First, the great desert of the Antipodes.

Australia is best described as a plateau whose interior is depressed and barren. In other words, it is like a vast saucer — high around the edges and low in the middle — and geologically it is claimed to be one of the oldest existing land masses. Apart from Antarctica, it was the last considerable territory to be discovered and the exploration of its coastline was not completed until 1831–1836, when Darwin finished the job in the *Beagle*. Years before that, however, men were already pushing into the interior — hard, solitary, wandering men with an irresistible urge to get up and go.

One such was Charles Sturt. Born in India in 1795, he fought in the Peninsular War against Napoleon and migrated to Australia in 1827. At this time, except for isolated settlements in the coastal regions, one of which was the penal colony at Botany Bay, the continent was inhabited only by the nomadic aborigine and virtually unknown. In New South Wales one of the many things that puzzled the settlers was a number of rivers that flowed away from the sea into the interior. What happened to them? Where did they go? In 1828, Sturt took off to find out.

Starting with the Murrumbidgee River, he followed it to its junction with the Murray and then traced the

Murray to its mouth in Lake Alexandrina, and the questions were answered.

Sturt continued to wander, his discoveries contributing significantly to the knowledge of the new land and its development; but for him, it was the wandering that mattered, the vast emptiness of the Australian interior that pulled him. Always he had to go on beyond the known and at last in 1844, he achieved what was for him the ultimate by penetrating to the geographic center of the continent.

What drove him and others like him? They came to Australia at the beginning and the best of it was theirs for the taking. Why did they choose instead to endure hardship and court death in that terrifying interior? Superficially the answer is obvious; they were looking for a better place and room to breathe as more and more people uprooted themselves from Europe and settled on the coastal strip. To these adventurers Australia was the *promised land*. For years past, the geographers and cosmologists had been dreaming of this vast continent in the southern ocean, and successive generations of mariners had sought it. Now it was found and it had to be fabulously rich and fertile, flowing with milk and honey, for that was how the legend described it; and while the southeast corner — New South Wales and Victoria — was a pretty fair place in which to settle, it was argued there must be more of it and better elsewhere. It was as simple as that. But there was something else that had nothing to do with material gain, something in the nature of the men — for though winning nothing, they still kept on at it.

Edward John Eyre was another of the breed and perhaps the best known of them all. On arriving in Australia, he took up land on the lower Murray River and in 1839 began probing into the country north of Spencer's Gulf, ostensibly in search of good grazing ground. Rumor had it that one particular valley in the region led to fertile highlands but what he eventually found was Lake Torrens, which he named. It was a grim place and his own description of it cannot be bettered.

> To the north-west [he wrote], and extending to the west as far as the eye could reach, was to be seen a very broad glittering stripe of what seemed to be water, but which I am inclined to think was not water, but only the dry and glazed bed of where water had lodged — and of very great extent. Nowhere could be seen the least sign of grass or water; the hills before me were high, barren, and rocky, and there were no gum trees or other indications of water emanating from them to be seen anywhere — the whole was barren and arid looking in the extreme, and as I gazed on the dismal scene before me I felt assured I had approached the vast and dreary desert of the interior, or, it might be, was verging on the confines of some inland water, whose sterile and desolate shores seem to forbid the traveller's approach.

This first and materially fruitless journey was financed by Eyre himself, but on returning to Adelaide, on the south coast, he quickly found backing for another expedition. The economics are interesting. Using packhorses for transport, he planned to take his food on the hoof, and to this end he bought twelve sheep in Port Lincoln which cost him 2 pounds. (At that time, the British pound was equivalent to approximately 5 dollars, the shilling to 25 cents.) But for nine horses the price was 682 pounds, 10 shillings. Even so, the total cost of the expedition was precisely 1391 pounds, 9 shillings, 7 pence — no more. Of this the government of the colony subscribed 100 pounds, the colonists raised 582 pounds, 4 shillings, 9 pence among them, and the sum of 28 pounds was brought in by the ultimate sale of surviving equipment. The balance of 680 pounds, 15 shillings, 10 pence Eyre dug out of his own pocket. This action is indicative of the kind of itch that was on him.

Returning to Lake Torrens, Eyre now went along its eastern side, making a closer examination on the way. He even rode six miles in toward its center, turning back only when the horses were bogged to the belly. This confirmed his earlier surmise that the area was a vast salt marsh; and pushing on, he came into what is now known as the Lake Eyre basin, "the driest and most desert area in Australia," and eventually to Lake Eyre itself. It was Lake Torrens all over again, only bigger, and it formed an impassable barrier across his path.

Backtracking to get a new line, he then crossed the Flinders Ranges and from the high ground saw another salt lake in his way about forty miles off, which was subsequently named Lake Frome. Balked again, he tried a third time, heading northeastward, and finally arrived at a place from which he saw more impassable lakes about twenty miles ahead. Literally surrounded now by desert and salt pan, he named the spot Mount Hopeless and called it a day.

Most men thus foiled would have gone home and put their feet up, but not Eyre. Instead, he sent the main body of his expedition back to Adelaide and headed west with the idea of striking the shoreline in the vicinity of Fowlers Bay and following it around the Great Australian Bight to Albany in Western Australia.

This was a journey that tested him to the limit and he had to pull out all the stops — endurance, resourcefulness, persistence, courage, and supreme self-confidence — to make it. Few men of any generation would have tried it and most of those would have turned back at some stage and likely enough gone under. For him there was no turning back; he had to get to Albany or die trying. He was plagued by dust storms, horseflies, hunger, and, above all else, thirst. Twice he went over 150 miles between water holes and one by one his animals — both packhorses and sheep — died of dehydration and lack of fodder. On top of this, he suffered from severe frosts at night, not being equipped to withstand such low temperatures. Then in the third month of his wandering, when everything except his driving will to go on seemed lost, he made contact with a French whaler anchored offshore. She took him aboard and he stayed fourteen days, resting and living fat for a change. Subsequently he named the place where she lay Rossiter Bay in honor of the master, who offered to take him back to Adelaide. Refusing the offer and resisting all entreaties, he set off again and three weeks later walked into Albany in a rainstorm. Everybody naturally wanted to make a fuss over him, but he would have none of it, and, after a glass of hot brandy, a bath, and a change of clothes, he returned to Adelaide. In his own words:

> Finding that a vessel would shortly sail for Adelaide, I at once engaged my passage, and proceeded to make arrangements for leaving King George's Sound.

In 1846, Eyre was appointed Governor General of New Zealand, and that put an end to his overlanding.

In spite of these wide-ranging journeys of men like Sturt and Eyre, however, Australia was in the main still unknown, and the old milk-and-honey myths about it persisted. Consequently, the next generation of wanderers still used the search for the *promised land* as the excuse and justification for their inability to stay put. They concentrated on the challenging enterprise of crossing the continent from south to north. Among them, the best-known name is Robert O'Hara Burke.

If anybody was ever smitten with wanderlust, he was. Born in Ireland, he was educated in Belgium and then went to Austria, where he joined the army. At twenty he was strutting it with the rank of captain; but eight years later he was back in Ireland enlisting in the Royal Irish Constabulary. After five years in the land of his birth, he pulled up his stakes and took off once more. This time he landed in Melbourne and again became a policeman — one imagines because he had to eat and no better way of satisfying the need presented itself. He stuck it out for seven years and then, opting out for the last time, tried to force the transcontinental route to the north; and with two companions — Wills and Gray — died on the way.

Burke was followed in 1862 by John McDouall Stuart who completed the journey. His achievement is both consolidated and commemorated by the Stuart Highway, a thousand miles of paved road linking Alice Springs in the center of the continent with Darwin on its northern shore. Incidentally, another thousand miles of paved road now runs south from Alice through the Lake Eyre Basin all the way to Adelaide, and this gives some idea of the emptiness in which these men roamed.

Ten years after Stuart came Giles. By this time a telegraph line spanned the continent from north to south and the areas of settlement in Western Australia were growing rapidly, but between the telegraph line and the settled areas there was still a thousand miles of unknown country about which men were asking the same old questions. Giles supplied the answers.

Born at Bristol and educated at Christ's Hospital, London, Giles went to Australia as a young man, and Madigan considers him to be one of the greatest explorers of his time. His first attempt to reach the Swan River settlements from the telegraph line was made with one companion, using horses for transport, in 1872. Keeping in or about latitude 25 degrees south, he discovered and named such features as Mount Solitary and Mount Peculiar, Carmichael and Deering Creeks, and a lake which he called Amadeus. West of the lake he failed to find water and was forced to retreat. But he had proved his quality and in 1873, he was off again, financed this time by a consortium of Victorian gentlemen. Even the South Australian government now loosened its purse strings to help him, but only slightly. It squeezed out 250 pounds, of which Giles said: "My poverty and not my will consented to accept so mean a gift."

On this second journey, Giles was accompanied by a friend of his English schooldays, a man called Tietkens, and again he relied on horses for transport. Altogether the expedition mustered four men and twenty-four horses. The idea was to force a passage of the desert country in a latitude south of Lake Amadeus. Traveling along the 26th parallel, Giles reached longitude 125 degrees 40 minutes east and was again driven back by the complete absence of water inside the range he could cover without it. Nevertheless, he felt no inclination to give up. Instead he went north for about 120 miles and again struck westward on or about the 24th parallel. With him went a young man named Gibson who had ambitions about being an overlander. Starting from a base camp established beside permanent water in the Rawlinson Range, they traveled 20 miles to the next water hole, which they called Circus Water. Here they filled two five-gallon kegs, which were cached another 60 miles farther on. At this point the pack animals were turned loose to make their own way back and, with one horse each, the two men slogged on across a spinifex and sandhill desert for another day in which they covered 38 miles. Then Gibson's horse broke down, and their only hope of survival was to backtrack to the cached kegs. Taking turns to ride and walk, leading the foundered horse, they had covered only eight miles when the exhausted animal lay down and died. And there they were — 30 miles from the kegs and 90 from the nearest water hole with one horse between them. Giles didn't hesitate for a moment. There was only one thing to do and he did it, sending Gibson on ahead with the horse, and himself starting the trek back to the base camp on foot.

It was a terrifying prospect for any man to face — 110 miles alone in that wilderness without food or water — but Giles never seemed to doubt he would make it. By the afternoon of the next day, he had reached the kegs, of which Gibson had left one together with a pound of dried horseflesh, but no water bag. This meant carrying the keg which itself weighed 15 pounds and now contained two gallons of water, making the total burden 35 pounds in the most awkward shape any load could come.

On he went, carrying the keg. The meat was soon gone but he made the water last five days, at the end of which he was twenty miles from Circus Water. Walking through the night, he arrived at the water hole next morning at daybreak. There he had the luck to catch and kill a young wallaby, eating it raw, "fur, skin, bones, skull and all." Resting up through the day, he got going again at sundown and reached the base camp next morning — eight days after the death of Gibson's horse. Gibson himself was never seen or heard of again, though a prolonged search was made, led by Giles himself. It was concluded that for some reason he had left the tracks he was following back and never regained them. His name stands on the map over the area where he died — Gibson Desert.

After such an experience and so desperately narrow an escape, most men would have pushed their luck no further; but Giles stayed with the problem he had dreamed up for himself and between 1874 and 1876 made the crossing from Adelaide to Perth in latitude 30 degrees south. This still left too much unknown for his peace of mind, and he finally recrossed the other way in latitude 24 degrees south, using camels.

The sad thing about Giles is that the country he traversed was so desolate and waterless that, as Madigan puts it, "settlement has never followed up his tracks," and he is almost forgotten. The implication, of course, is that in terms of profit and loss his efforts were wasted; but seeing the man in retrospect, it is extremely doubtful if he would, even in his worst moments, endorse that judgment.

With modern transport, society no longer needs men like Giles and in the natural order of things, they should have disappeared from the scene long since; but they persist and nowhere more so than in the Australian outback. They are the solitary prospectors for whom the search matters more than the find, the lonely optimists searching for gold in derelict mine workings, and the sundowners — those true "sons of Martha" — wandering forever with no goal and no urge in them except the itch to keep going. The ostensible purpose is gone and only the overriding need to be themselves remains; but though they open up no new territory and create no material wealth, though in a sense they are parasitic on society, it could be that they are making their biggest contribution ever just in being different and keeping alive man's essential individuality.

Next, the Sahara. Of all the world's deserts, this is the biggest. Stretching from the Mediterranean south to the Sudan and from the Atlantic Ocean east to the Red Sea, it covers three and a half million square miles of North Africa and contains both the Libyan and Nubian deserts within its boundaries. Of this area, two and a half million square miles is actual wasteland. Contrary to popular belief, it is neither low-lying nor flat, but an elevated plateau that never drops below sea level and rises to mountains of 8000 feet that are snow-capped in winter. The Mountains of Aïr reach to 6000 feet and there are extensive ridges, notably the Tassili of the Adjjer, which is 300 miles long and has a mean altitude of 4500 feet.

The dominant feature of the terrain is the sand hill, covering one ninth of the total area. A single complex of these runs continuously from Cape Blanco on the Atlantic coast to a point south of Tunisia 1300 miles to the eastward. Elsewhere there are areas of stony desert, others of water-worn pebbles, and others again of soft sand, wind-blown into high shifting dunes.

The frightening thing about the Sahara Desert is that to a large extent it is man-made, and still drying up. The nomad, cutting down trees and shrubs for firing, and his goats eating off the young vegetation, have denuded vast stretches in the last 1300 years. Consequently the area is studded with deserted and ruined cities, crisscrossed with abandoned caravan routes and, in spite of the reclamation projects of visionaries, becoming more deserted than ever before. Enormous areas are completely void of all vegetation, one such being the Libyan Desert, which stretches unbroken for 800 miles southward from the Siwah Oasis without a growing thing.

The summer temperatures are among the highest encountered anywhere on earth, reaching to over 120 degrees F. There are sometimes severe frosts, but the winter mean is about 60 degrees F. The land is virtually rainless and what water it holds is all subterranean.

Like every other empty space in the world, the Sahara has now been cut down to size by the automobile and the airplane; but up to half a century ago it was as good a place as any for a man to lose himself in. The opportunity to do so in a big way was offered by the French in 1831 when they organized their *Régiment Étranger*, more familiarly known as the Foreign Legion. The concept was fine — an organization within which a man could deliberately abandon his identity; a community of males like a monastic order but dedicated to action instead of meditation and offering as a bonus a fifty-fifty chance of a quick exit by a Bedouin bullet or heat stroke and thirst. But the whole idea, like the history of the Sahara, has been hopelessly romanticized by the movie epic and popular fiction. Consequently, the skeptic is inclined to dismiss the glamorous Foreign Legion as a bunch of toughies and their mystique as an adman's gimmick.

Nevertheless, for a thousand years and more, men have been accepting the challenge of the Sahara. In 1826, a Major Alexander Laing crossed it southward to Timbuktu. Other English names associated with it are John Davidson (1836), John Richardson (1845), Colonel Flatters (1861), and Captain A. Buchanan who traveled by camel from Kano to Tuggurt in 1922; but nobody has ever been so completely one with this particular desert as Antoine de Saint-Exupéry, the French fighter pilot. For him the Sahara was no challenge, no mere proving ground over which to test his courage and endurance; it was a love affair, intensely passionate, but relatively brief; for, though on one occasion he did experience the torment of thirst in the Libyan Desert, he made no great journeys except by air and learned most of what he knew about the wasteland while in charge of an aircraft-staging post at Cape Juby in Morocco.

Born in 1900 into a relatively impoverished but well-connected family, Saint-Exupéry was a nonconformer almost from his first breath, and in the whole of his life he was never contented with things as they were. But it would be too easy to put him down simply as a congenital dissenter. He was that, all right; but much more besides. Even as a boy he could not be labeled, and as a man he has been pigeonholed into a dozen different categories and stayed put in none of them. Nicknaming him *Pique-la-lune* — Moonpecker — because of his turned-up nose and habit of stargazing, his schoolmates wrote him off as an eccentric; but even in those days there was at the heart of him a simple and all-powerful urge to self-fulfillment that accounted for and made sense of everything he did.

He had a passion for wide horizons and at the age of twelve, after being taken up in an airplane by Jules Védrines, he tried to get airborne on his own by fitting wings to his bicycle. It was around this time that the deeper, introspective side of his nature began to assert itself and the potential brilliance of his intellect to show, particularly in the philosophy classes. At seventeen he had rejected all religious teaching and from then on he sought for understanding and truth wherever his instincts told him they might be found.

At twenty he did the usual term of compulsory military service and even then he had a leaning toward solitude, renting a room of his own outside the barracks and eating in restaurants rather than in the company mess. At twenty-three, he was flying, partly for the fun of it, but mainly for the "ineffable joy of solitude in the sky." Back in civilian life, while working in turn as a bookkeeper and traveling car salesman, he became a reserve pilot in the air force. Marcel Migeo says of him in this period:

> Once in the air he was happy; nothing weighed him down, nothing depressed him, he felt renewed and without burdens again. Altitude meant something more than flying in the air above the earth; it meant, for him, leaving behind the meanness he often encountered in his fellowmen, banishing all the scurvy tricks and intrigues and demeaning acts, big and little, of daily life . . . so purifying and revivifying was the solitude of the sky.

It has been said he was difficult and too demanding and it is true that he deliberately withdrew from some people; but there was a reason:

> It hurts me when I do not find what I look for in someone [he said], and I am always disappointed and disgusted when I discover that a mentality I had believed to be interesting is noth-

ing but a mechanism easy to take apart. I have
a grudge then, against that person. I'm eliminat-
ing a lot of people from my life, men and
women, I simply can't help it.

In 1924, Saint-Ex, as he became known to his in-
timates, joined the select band of pilots who under the
aegis of the Latécoère Air Line were pioneering air-
mail routes across Spain to North Africa and thence to
South America. But for him, flying was not "a sov-
ereign vocation"; rather, it was a means to an end, a
way to spiritual and mental freedom. His vocation was
living. It was flying, however, that brought him to Juby
and the Sahara.

His task there was to keep the planes in the air and
to rescue any that came to grief in the desert. It involved brief periods of intense activity sometimes
fraught with great danger, and long spells of quiet and
stillness when he meditated and recorded his responses
to the desert.

In his own phrase, he "succumbed to the desert at
first sight," and he exulted in its solitude. There was
about it for him a mystique comparable with that of the
monastic life, and writing of a night spent by a wrecked
plane, he says:

> . . . we were infinitely poor. Wind, sand, and
> stars. The austerity of Trappists . . . a hand-
> ful of men who possessed nothing in the world
> but their memories were sharing invisible riches.

It was his belief that self-fulfillment can only be attained by meeting and overcoming obstacles. "The one thing that matters is the effort," he wrote in *The Wisdom of the Sands*, and again in *Wind, Sand and Stars*. "It is not money that can procure for us that vision of the world won through hardship." What most men called happiness he saw as stagnation. The desert demanded renunciation — life within its confines was always primitive, often difficult, and sometimes dangerous, and that suited him fine. Physical courage he discounted, seeing it as a complex of feelings not in themselves wholly praiseworthy: ". . . a touch of anger, a spice of vanity, a lot of obstinacy and a tawdry sporting thrill," but he believed there could be no worthwhile passion, no enrichment of the soul that did not involve suffering.

When his novel, *Night Flight*, was awarded the Prix Femina in 1931, he was flying the mail on the Casablanca-Dakar section and got leave to return to Paris to receive the prize.

> When he got out of the plane [writes his biographer and friend, Marcel Migeo], a three days' growth of beard covered his face . . . and the beard was spattered with oil from the engines, not wiped off during the twenty hours of flight; on his feet were a pair of old canvas espadrilles; his trousers were as stained as they were ragged; he was wearing no shirt, and his old navy blue raincoat was tied round his waist by a string . . .

That was Antoine de Saint-Exupéry — a lonely man who cared nothing for rules but valued solitude, loved people and grieved over their inability to communicate with each other.

> Within reach of me [he wrote], apparently, are men cloistered in a monastery or in a laboratory or in a love affair, but in reality they are as beyond reach as if they were in the most remote parts of Tibet, no, farther still, for no journey I could ever take would bring me close to them . . .

He also loved silence and wrote of it in *The Wisdom of the Sands*:

> I will indite a hymn to thee, O Silence . . . In thy embrace I fold the city viewed from the mountain-top, when night has stilled its rumbling wheels and clanging anvils and the tumult of its streets, and all things float becalmed in a bowl of shadows. For silence is God's cloak spread out upon man's restlessness, and in silence He steeps and soothes their fretful hearts . . .

Unlike most flying men, he believed arriving somewhere was the least important thing about traveling. He saw any journey as a quest for distance; and to his mind distance was not to be found. "It melts away," he wrote, "and escape has never led anywhere . . ."

He traveled a great deal after the Sahara interlude,

but it is doubtful that he ever got much satisfaction out of it. Léon Werth, who was closer to him than anybody else ever got, described him as "the most limpid and at the same time the most troubled of men . . . He was imprisoned but never at rest." On July 31, 1944, he set off on a reconnaissance mission from Corsica, from which he never returned. It is generally assumed he was shot down by a German fighter plane and died in the sea.

Finally Arabia, which the Arabs call Jazirat-al-Arab. Translated, this means simply "peninsula of the Arabs"; and peninsula it is, lying between 12°45′ and 34°50′ north latitude and 30°30′ and 60°00′ east longitude. Thus the farthest one can travel there in a beeline is roughly 1500 miles north and south and 1250 miles east and west. Its total area is 1.2 million square miles, of which almost half is desert.

As already noted, within the confines of the desert portion there is every kind of terrain from high rocky plateau through sand hill and stony wilderness to windswept dunes and salt flats well below sea level.

Unlike Australia, so recently discovered and opened up by the white man, Arabia has been known as long as man has been aware of anything, and the European has been in it as settler, conqueror, honored guest, or footloose wanderer since way back before the Romans. They were there, of course, just as they were everywhere else in the known world, and according to Ptolemy they were particularly familiar with the coastal regions and the interior of the northern part. The first known Englishman to travel Arabia was Joseph Pitts in or around 1690; but there must have been many, many others who for one reason or another never got into the record. More recently, the big names in Arabian travel are J. L. Burckhardt (1784–1817), Sir Richard Burton (1801–1890), C. M. Doughty (1843–1926), Wilfred Scawen Blunt (1840–1922), T. E. Lawrence (1888–1935), Bertram Thomas (b. 1892), and H. St. John Philby (b. 1885). The last three belong very much to the twentieth century. They demonstrate the working of the strange spell this vast emptiness casts over the mind and heart of the man of our time who craves for nothing but room in which to be himself.

In spite of the lure and the numbers who had fallen for it down the centuries, by 1930 no more than twenty Europeans had truly penetrated to the heart of Arabia; and the Great Southern Desert, otherwise known as the Empty Quarter and called by the Arabs Rub' al Khali, remained untrodden except by the Bedouin. It appeared on the map as a blank area half the size of Europe and was then described as "the last considerable *terra incognita*." It presented a challenge that haunted a number of people, but none more than Bertram Thomas and Harry St. John Philby.

Described as an orientalist, Thomas served as Political Officer in Iraq and Assistant British Representative in Trans-Jordan, then became Wazir to the Sultan of Muscat and Oman. He had a passion for wandering in Arabia and was very much respected by the Bedouin

and other nomads. T. E. Lawrence wrote of him in
the foreword to *Arabia Felix*:

> Few men are able to close an epoch. We cannot
> know the first man who walked the inviolate
> earth for newness' sake; but Thomas is the last;
> and he did his journey in the antique way,
> by pain of his camel's legs, single-handed, at
> his own time and cost. He might have flown an
> aeroplane, sat in a car or rolled over in a tank.
> Instead he has snatched at the twenty-third hour,
> feet's last victory and set us free . . .

Thomas was well fitted for desert wandering. In his
own phrase, he "enjoyed advantages." His thirteen
years of service in the country had given him a very
special and peculiar knowledge of tribal dialects; he
knew the Arab ways and had adapted to the climate.

The idea of crossing the Rub' al Khali had been in his
mind for years; but he knew the British official attitude
and thought processes too well either to publicize his
desire or seek permission to fulfill it. Sir Richard Burton
had been refused such permission in 1852 and nothing
had changed very much since. The authorities were still
opposed to anybody's making that kind of journey. As
they saw it, the spin-off, if any, could not possibly
justify the risks involved. So, as Thomas puts it,
". . . my plans were conceived in darkness, my journeys heralded only by my disappearances, paid for by
myself and executed under my own auspices."

In the winter of 1927, he began the project with a

reconnaissance which took him by camel from the southeast corner of the peninsula 600 miles along the southern borders of the empty quarter to Dhufar. He wore Bedouin dress, spoke only in the local dialect, cut out both alcohol and tobacco, and lived in every way as one of the people. The following winter, starting from Dhufar, he explored the steppe country to the north, covering 200 miles and reaching to the edge of the sands. Then on October 4, 1930, he slipped out of Muscat under cover of darkness and was picked up three miles offshore by a tanker bound out of the Gulf toward Aden. The tanker transferred him to a dhow, which landed him at Risut. From Risut he rode by camel to Dhufar, arriving there on October 8.

There, after three months of patient waiting, he made contact with the Rashid — the only Bedouin tribe familiar with the Rub' al Khali — and gathered together a party of 40 led by Shaikh Salih bin Kalut.

> I looked down into the fort courtyard [says Thomas describing their arrival], upon forty dainty riding camels and as many ragged Badawin that had come two hundred miles at my secret bidding out of the sands of Rub' al Khali . . .

Swearing the Shaikh to secrecy, Thomas revealed his heart's desire. It was to cross the desert from sea to sea, coming out wherever it was possible — Riyadh, Abu Dhabi, or Bahrain — and Shaikh Salih agreed to see him through.

The journey, it was decided, would have to be done in four relays, and the organization was tricky. The amount of food carried — butter, rice, dates, and flour — had to be precisely calculated, as had the number of men, which was fixed at forty, to be reduced first to thirty, then twenty, and finally fifteen. Besides the riding camels they would have at the outset fifteen pack camels. Thomas also carried three thousand silver dollars with which to pay his way.

They set out from Dhufar on December 10, Shaikh Salih putting their chances of success at no more than even. Thomas, recording the estimate, did not think it necessary to add that failure in this context was synonymous with death. Their route led them up over Jabal Qara, a range of mountains rising to 3000 feet within twenty miles of the sea, on the northern slopes of which the frankincense shrub grows and is milked like the rubber tree. The top of this ridge marked the northern limit of settlement; beyond it the limestone gave way to a wilderness of sandstone that took six days of marching to traverse and brought them to the edge of the sands.

At the water hole called Shisur, they were ninety miles in from the coast, 935 feet above sea level, and five days out from the last water. Ahead of them lay a stretch of seven or eight days to the next.

On December 24 they entered dune country:

> Before us rose red mountains of sand . . . a vast
> ocean of billowing sands, here tilted into sudden

frowning heights, and there falling to gentle valleys merciful for camels, though without a scrap of verdure in view. Dunes of all sizes, unsymmetrical in relation to one another . . . rise tier upon tier like a mighty mountain system . . .

They started across this stretch called Urup-adh-Dhahiya on Christmas morning. The sand was soft and the slopes precipitous, and the camels sank knee-deep at every step in spite of their great pads. Thomas reckoned no horse could ever have got through such territory, and a car would have been useless in it. But so far as he was concerned the effort was worthwhile:

> There were moments when we came suddenly upon a picture of sublime grandeur, an immense and noble plastic architecture, an exquisite purity of colour, old rose-red, under the cloudless sky and brilliant light . . .

The next water hole was Khor Dhahiya, after which the party, reduced to twenty men as planned, entered the sands of Dakaka heading for the well called Shanna. There the final objective was fixed. It was to be Doha in the Qatar Peninsula on the Persian Gulf, which left them 330 miles to go as the crow flies across a "barren ocean of interior sands . . ." Leaving Shanna on January 10, they reached the water hole of Bainhat on the thirteenth and were into the sand region of Sanam, "white and rolling in a gentle swell," on the nineteenth. This is the area famous for the sweetness of its water holes and their abnormal depth, the average being about eleven fathoms and the deepest up to seventeen.

Another three days brought them into the red sand-hills of Ubaila, and there they encountered a succession of sandstorms which tried them sorely. The wind was northerly and the night temperature down to 37 degrees F. They pushed on, however, and on January 28 arrived at Banaiyan, which was no mere water hole, but a real well and stone-lined. It was only eighty miles now to the sea.

After a whole day at Banaiyan, resting men and camels, they went on into an area where steppes covered with "gravel of jasper and gypsum, pebbles of black, white, red and green," alternated with strips of salt pan and rolling sandhills. There was vegetation here and wildlife also, for they saw the tracks of hyena and wildcat.

The going was relatively easy now, though the risk of being attacked by marauding tribesmen had increased. The solitude, however, remained unbroken and on February 2, Thomas saw the waters of the Persian Gulf from a hilltop. Three days later, on the fifth, the party arrived at Doha, and one of the greatest desert journeys ever attempted was completed.

By then Harry St. John Philby had already started what was to be the second crossing of the Empty Quarter.

Next to T. E. Lawrence, St. John Philby is perhaps the best known of all twentieth-century European wanderers in Arabia. Like so many other seekers after

empty places, he was a traveler almost from his birth
— which took place in Ceylon. From there he went to
England to be educated at Westminster School and
Cambridge, then in 1908 joined the Indian Civil Service,
eventually becoming political officer at d'Amara in what
was then Mesopotamia and is now Iraq. In 1917 and
into 1918 he led a British political mission to Central
Arabia and from 1921 to 1924 was the British Representative in Trans-Jordan. Long before this, the Arabian Desert had him hooked and for keeps. His first
big journey was made in 1918, when he spent a whole
year wandering the northern boundaries of the Empty
Quarter from Hasa to the great Wadi of the Dawasir.
From then on, he wanted nothing but the privilege of
crossing the Rub' al Khali:

> For fifteen years [he says] my life has been
> dominated by a single idea, a single ambition —
> rather perhaps a single obsession. Faithfully, fa-
> natically and relentlessly through all those years,
> I have stalked the quarry . . .

In 1924, planning to satisfy what he called "the in-
satiable craving within me to penetrate the recesses of
that Empty Quarter . . ." he got as far as Jidda on the
Red Sea, but was struck down with dysentery and had
to abandon the attempt before it even got going.

Then he settled in Mecca, where "the great peace of
Islam slowly and surely descended" upon him. He became a Moslem but still pursued his dream. Another

seven years passed before he got the blessing and the backing of King Ibn Saud, and by that time Bertram Thomas was already nearly a month out from Dhufar, heading northward into the void.

There was room enough for both of them in the Rub' al Khali, however, and for a lot more besides, and on January 6, 1932, Philby left Hufuf, which lies to the north of the emptiness and between Riyadh and the Persian Gulf. The party consisted of eleven men and a dog with fifteen camels "festooned with water-skins and garlands of raw dry meat . . ." and their staple diet was to be dates dipped in butter and washed down with coffee. The route was southerly through the oasis of Jabrin and the wells of Maqainama, Bir Fadhil, Tuwairifa, Wabar and Naifa to Shanna which they reached on February 20. From Shanna, on February 22 they headed westward into the desert, but after four days of slogging were forced to turn back because of the poor condition of both men and beasts.

Returning to Naifa, they holed up there for five days to recuperate, and then set off again into the 400-mile waterless stretch that lay between them and the wells of Latwa, near Sulaiyil. The worst stint was the great gravel plain of Abu Bahr, "protruding southward from the Summan steppe like a vast promontory of *Terra firma* in the midst of the great sand ocean."

> Vast and naked and flat it spread out before us to a sea-like horizon, with only an islet of dunes far out in its midst to the northwest to break its

impressive monotony . . . Abu Bahr . . . was wholly and simply true to its name — an ocean, unruffled, serene and silent, without a mark of any kind to guide the traveller . . .

They made the wells of Latwa on March 14 and Sulaiyil two days later, proceeding thence to Mecca and thus completing Philby's third crossing of Arabia. He was not in any way cast down by the fact that Thomas had beaten him to the traverse of the Rub' al Khali. Rivalry had no place in his make-up and it was never a competition for either of them. Philby's own words, "Let a man be true in his intentions and his efforts to fulfil them and the point is gained whether he succeed or not," went for both. Of his companions, parted with forever at Mecca, he would, he said,

> . . . remember the good and forget the evil of our strange association in an enterprise which had filled my dreams for 14 years and racked their nerves for as many weeks. To them and the great beasts that bore us — hungering and thirsting but uncomplaining — the credit of a great adventure . . .

For himself, he was content. "I have done enough to set my soul at rest," he wrote, ". . . and mine is the pleasure of telling the tale."

What was it that made these men — St. John Philby and Bertram Thomas — haunt that wilderness and risk death inside its boundaries? T. E. Lawrence, whose own ostensible purpose for being in Arabia was to create a nation out of an agglomeration of nomadic, warring tribes, had something to say about excuses for traveling there:

> Our feebler selves [he wrote] dare not be Arabians for Arabia's sake . . . One will fix latitudes . . . another collect plants or insects (not to eat, but to bring home), a third make war, which is coals to Newcastle. We fritter our allegiances and loyalties.

So Thomas declared his aim was to explore and map the Rub' al Khali; to this end he was equipped with chronometers and other precision instruments. Philby, however, made no excuses. He went there simply because he wanted to, which for him was sufficient reason, and indicates how widely different the two men were. Yet there are three things they had in common and shared with Lawrence.

First, they had a passion for solitude and silence with everything that implies — the habit of meditation, the love of nature untouched by man, the hatred of crowds and of being pushed around, a strict code of personal conduct, self-imposed, along with the total rejection of other men's rules, which made them draw a sharp distinction between the discipline they admired and the authority they despised and flouted whenever it suited them to do so.

Second, they found greater satisfaction and a more subtle and lasting pleasure in denying their appetites and desires than could ever come out of indulging them. So Thomas accepted the discomforts and hardships, the poverty and privation of the Bedouin. Philby went even further and deliberately abstained from water for weeks on end, drinking only a little tea and some camel's milk.

With Lawrence, this self-denial became almost a cult, and some writers have seen it as a form of masochism. There is no doubt, however, that he practiced it as a virtue:

> In Arabia, where superfluities lacked, the temptation of necessary food lay always on men. Each morsel which passed their lips might, if they were not watchful, become a pleasure. Luxuries might be as plain as running water or a shady tree, whose rareness and misuse often turned them into lusts . . .

And for years he schooled himself by what he called "constant carelessness," stuffing down all the food he could hold one day, then going the next two, three, or even four days without eating at all. In time he arrived at a state of mind wherein he "felt neither hunger nor surfeit" and like the Arabs, marched dry between wells, drinking "greatly today for the thirst of yesterday and of tomorrow." So too with sleep. For him it was the ultimate pleasure, which he denied himself until he could make a long succession of laborious night marches "without undue fatigue." But Lawrence believed *will* was paramount and it could well be that the need to prove it to himself was at the bottom of everything he did. Thus he *willed* himself to do without food, without water, without sleep; and when he felt he had betrayed the Arabs, he *willed* himself to lose his identity — the one thing everybody else is trying so desperately hard to find. Maybe he even *willed* his death; he certainly courted it.

The third thing these men shared was the kind of solitude they sought. Basically it was of the mind and emotions, had nothing to do with isolation and was only incidentally physical. So, even while indulging themselves in it, they could still desire community and even enjoy it; but it had to be of a special kind — one that made no demands except the purely physical, one within which they could feel a sense of belonging and yet remain themselves inviolate and alone; and it had to have the right values. Thus Thomas:

> . . . to one who has experienced them, who has learned to talk with his only companions for months on end — rude and unlettered brigands of the desert though they be — and to admire some of their virile qualities, the camel-back and the long marches go to make the magic of Arabia.

Thus Philby, exulting at the end of a spell of twenty-seven hours without coffee:

> That was a supreme test of Arab virtue, and our great march across Abu Bahr revealed both the

Arab and his camel at their very best. It was indeed a stupendous performance, just such a feat as they sing of in their ballads and vaunt in the epics of their ancient chivalry. It was the crowning glory of our whole adventure, though a crown of thorns very painful in the making.

And thus T. E. Lawrence, saying nothing, but renouncing the role of national hero for the anonymity of a number and the cheerless poverty of the barrack room; rejecting the society of the cultured and well-to-do for the clumsy but disinterested affection of the underprivileged.

II

North Atlantic Nomads

THE MOST EASILY accessible empty spaces in the world are its oceans, and none of them has attracted so many loners as the Atlantic. It is a sizable place at least by earthly standards, stretching from latitude 70 degrees north to 40 degrees south and dividing Europe and Africa from the Americas, the Old World from the New. Its total area is 24 million square miles; the concern here is with that 14 million of it lying to the north of the Equator. This expanse, usually referred to as the North Atlantic (though sailormen call it the Western Ocean), has a width varying from 4500 miles between Florida and the coast of Morocco, and a mere 1600 miles from the Guinea coast to the bulge of Brazil.

The North Atlantic is divided into four weather zones. Their limits vary, and the whole system has a seasonal oscillation of about 300 miles, reaching its most northerly position in July or August and its most southerly in January or February. The zones are:

The Doldrums: That part of the ocean lying in the equatorial trough of low pressure situated between the trade winds of the two hemispheres . . . The characteristic features of this zone are calms and light variable winds alternating with squalls, heavy rains, and thunderstorms.

Northeast Trade Winds: These are remarkable for their steadiness and persistence. They blow permanently and vary very little in direction, though considerably in force. The average strength is Beaufort 3 to 4 (gentle to moderate) but they can increase to 5 or 6 (fresh to strong) or lull to force 1 (light air).

Variables: A belt of winds varying in both direction and force and otherwise known as the horse latitudes.

Westerlies: This zone stretches from the northern edge of the variables to the southern rim of the Arctic. In it the winds are mainly westerly but the constant passage of depressions across the area causes a great deal of more or less local variation in direction and force. So on any one day in any given spot the wind might be from any direction and rate as anything from a light breeze to a full gale — which is a roundabout way of saying it is unpredictable.

There are three main currents in the North Atlantic — the North Equatorial Current and the Gulf Stream, which are warm, and the Labrador Current, which is cold. The Gulf Stream might well be considered the most remarkable feature of the area. It issues from the Gulf of Mexico and flows northward through the Straits of Florida and along the eastern seaboard of

North America to a point south of Newfoundland, where it becomes the Gulf Stream Drift and continues eastward to the coasts of western Europe. Emerging from the Gulf of Mexico, this great river in the sea has a temperature of about 80 degrees F and flows at an average speed of 80 miles a day; but both temperature and velocity diminish after it has turned to the eastward.

Leaving aside the weather, the risk of death from hunger, thirst, or exposure, and the possibility of the bottom's dropping out of his craft, the seafarer in the North Atlantic faces three special hazards. They are fog and bad visibility, such as that caused by driving snow; the risk of collision in the congested steamer tracks; and bergs that have broken off the Greenland icecap, drifting southward in the grip of the Labrador Current. On the half-million square miles of the Grand Bank south and east of Newfoundland, where the water shoals abruptly from over 2000 fathoms to under a hundred, these three dangers converge, along with the shipping lanes, and it is easy to think of healthier places in which to loiter. The list of disasters that have occurred here, topped by the loss of the unsinkable *Titanic* in 1912, is as long as man's memory of the place and the total of lives lost in them beyond computing.

There is considerable evidence that the Vikings, groping their way from Iceland via the Denmark Strait and Cape Farewell, crossed the Atlantic in the eleventh century; but the first truly documented passage was that of Christopher Columbus aboard the *Santa Maria* in 1492. He took seventy days over it and thought it was

China he had arrived at. In 1620 the Pilgrim Fathers in the *Mayflower* made a much longer voyage of it, being 106 days from Plymouth Sound to Plymouth, Massachusetts. Nowadays man moves faster, though no one knows exactly to what end, and the record for the modern liner measured from Bishop Rock Lighthouse to Ambrose Light-vessel off New York — a distance of 2906 miles — is well under four days.

The North Atlantic has always been different things to different men. To Columbus it was a magic paradox — the way to the East going west; to the Pilgrim Fathers and thousands after them, it was the road to spiritual freedom, to countless others the broad highway to the foot of the rainbow and a lusher life in the golden West; to the professional seaman, a hard, cold, wet way of earning a living for his wife and kids, to the amateur sailor, a constant challenge; and for the congenital loner, a solitude giving him advantages in regard to self-sufficiency and range neither desert nor mountaintop could ever match. Men have cut adrift into it aboard almost everything that floats, from a rubber dinghy upward; and in the second half of the nineteenth century, a succession of tough characters even rowed across it as a quick way to fame and fortune.

The first on record was the *Vision*, described by Jean Merrien as "a 14 foot dinghy rigged as a brigantine," although conjuring up a mental picture of such a thing must be beyond the power of anybody outside a lunatic asylum. The project was a circulation-boosting stunt, dreamed up and financed with the maximum of ballyhoo by the *New York Herald Tribune.* The *Vision,* sailing from New York on June 26, 1864, was sighted 45 miles east of Fire Island on the twenty-eighth and never heard of again. Two years later the *Nonpareil,* a craft constructed entirely of rubber, is reputed to have made it, but details of the feat are not available.

Ten years after the *Nonpareil* came the first solo crossing. It was made in a dory by a man called Johnson. Eighteen seventy-six was the centenary of the Declaration of Independence and Johnson was, above all other things, a patriot. He wanted to mark the occasion by a tremendous feat of courage and endurance that would symbolize the spirit of America, and he asked nothing for himself but the privilege of showing his boat at the Centenary Exhibition. The incredible thing is that he succeeded and took only forty-six days in which to do it. He had the westerly wind behind him all the way and that must have helped, but even so it was a fantastic achievement.

Like everybody else who ever did anything remarkable, Johnson had his imitators, and according to Merrien there were a number of other crossings and attempted crossings from west to east in the next few years, the most controversial being that claimed by the Andrews brothers in 1878. Their boat was a twelve-footer, partly decked, rigged with a standing lug and a jib on a long boom, and named *Dark Secret.* She eventually turned up in Le Havre, but, because she was never sighted on the way and arrived — both men and boat — in such excellent condition, some people suspected the voyage was a fake; that the brothers had in fact been picked up by some vessel just out of sight of land and carried across.

There was no doubt, however, about the Norwegians, Harbo and Samuelson, who rowed across west to east, in 1896. They too were backed — "sponsored," in the current idiom — by a newspaper, this time the *Police Gazette*, which provided the boat, then equipped and stored her. She was a whaler, seventeen foot nine over-all, clinker built and completely open except for a watertight locker at each end, designed to keep her afloat when she filled. The trip was pure show biz and the two men never pretended it was anything else. They thought they were going to make a fortune out of exhibiting themselves and their boat in the great cities of the world. All they had to do was get there and they were made for life.

The curious thing is the degree to which they had worked it all out. The basic factors were the length of stroke and the number of strokes per minute. Taking the first as 2½ yards and the second as 35 and making allowances for the wind — it would be fair for three quarters of the time and in their teeth for the rest — they expected to do 80 yards a minute, which works out to 57 miles a day. In the event they averaged 65 and reached the Scilly Islands on the fifty-fifth day out. Merrien calculates they made a total of 2,872,800 strokes of the oar on the crossing. Unlike the Andrews brothers, they were sighted five times on the way — first by the schooner *Jessie*, and next by the schooner *Leader* and the German steamer *Prince Bismarck*. Then, half-way across and thirty-nine days out, they were spoken by the Norwegian three-master, *Cito*. Finally, forty-eight days out and still 400 miles west of the Scillies, they were spoken by the *Eugen*, another Norwegian three-master.

Unhappily for the two would-be folk heroes, something else cropped up to crowd them out of the headlines, and when they arrived nobody wanted to know, not even the *Police Gazette*; so the fortune did not materialize and all they got out of it, excluding the calluses and overdeveloped biceps, was the ride.

After Harbo and Samuelson the bottom fell out of the market for transatlantic oarsmen; but it has regained a degree of buoyancy in recent times, largely through the toil and tears of a thirty-one-year-old Britisher, John Fairfax, who, and God alone knows why, wanted to be the first man to row across from east to west and solo. He had a boat, 23 feet long, specially designed for the job by one of the big names among amateur sailors, and called her *Britannia*. Starting from Las Palmas in the Canary Islands, on January 20, 1969, he headed for the Florida coast and calculated he would make it in roughly three months. Instead, he was exactly twice as long, reaching Fort Lauderdale, Florida, on July 19, after 180 days of rowing. Fairfax emerged from the adventure with a strong claim to be the most unflappable character of all time, and without his extraordinary phlegmatic attitude to the prolonged ordeal, it is doubtful if he would have survived. As it was, he stepped ashore at the end of it like a man coming in from an afternoon on the river.

Between the starry-eyed Norwegians and the ever cool Fairfax came the craziest of them all — a German seaman, Captain Romer, who in 1928 set out from the Canaries for the West Indies in a kayak. His craft was made of canvas on a wooden frame; it was 19 feet 6 inches long and 3 feet in the beam. The effort looked like a particularly cruel and stupid way of committing suicide; but after eighty-eight days of unimaginable suffering, Romer arrived at St. Thomas against all the odds and more dead than alive. What he had against himself was never revealed, but he was a real glutton for punishment, and after a spell recuperating in the hospital, he shoved off again, bound for New York. He was, however, asking too much of good fortune, though how, where, and why he met his end remains a mystery; we only know that he never got back in out of the cold.

Not one of the characters so far mentioned was cultivating solitude for its own sake. Whether the payoff was to be the fast buck or a glow of national pride, they were essentially fame-seekers. Even Romer comes into this category, his gimmick being to make the transatlantic voyage in the smallest and frailest craft currently used by man. But Alain Bombard, who crossed in 1953, drifting every inch of the way in a rubber dinghy, had a serious humanitarian purpose instead of a record in his sights, and there was no gimmickry at all about his achievement.

Bombard was a French scientist who, making a study

of marine disasters, was appalled by the number of people who survived the collision, fire, foundering, or what have you, only to perish miserably in the lifeboats before they could be picked up. As he saw it, their suffering and ultimate death from lack of food and drink and despair of a future was unnecessary, because everything they needed for survival, including hope, was there in the sea around them. What these people had really died of was ignorance, and he set out to enlighten future generations of shipwrecked mariners.

Isolated in his laboratory and experimenting only on himself, he proved the body can be sustained on sea water, judiciously drunk, at least long enough for a castaway to get around to catching fish. Thereafter, the fish, eaten raw, would provide in their juices all the moisture needed for survival. But laboratory proof was not enough; Bombard had to demonstrate his theory in practice, and this he set out to do.

Knowing that barrels and other trash dumped overboard off the bulge of Africa were caught up in the North Equatorial Current and carried across to the West Indies, he planned simply to become himself a bit of such flotsam. So, with nothing but what he stood up in, he cast off from the Canary Islands — no food, no water, no radio or other means of signaling for help, and no tools or equipment except what might be found in any man's pockets if he were frisked without warning. For him there was to be no way back; he was out on his own with nothing to sustain his body but his two hands and calculating brain, and only faith in his theory between him and madness. He had to start catching fish and/or collecting rainwater immediately, and the penalty for failing to keep on doing so would be death.

In the days of the sail, the area he traversed had been much frequented by ships, but steamers and motor vessels use other routes. Consequently, Bombard saw nothing for over seven weeks except the wildlife of the ocean — the odd bird circling overhead; the dolphin and bonito, curious as cats, pausing to examine him before continuing on their inscrutable way; and the small fry — plankton, flying fish, and anything else he could grab — that sustained him. Then on the fifty-third day out, he was sighted and spoken by the British steamer *Arakaka*, whose master invited him aboard. By this time Bombard had proved his point amply, and he allowed himself to accept a shower and a hot meal; but he refused all offers of a lift to the land, persuasive and persistent though they were. When he had washed and eaten, he went back to his dinghy to drift the rest of the way.

It took him another twelve days — sixty-five in all — and he spent the time when he wasn't fishing, regretting that brief spell of comfort and the meal of civilized food he had taken aboard the *Arakaka*. Both physically and psychologically he had learned to tolerate the diet of raw fish, to accept the taste of it in his mouth and the feel of it going down his gullet without retching. But now the mere thought of it made him ill and he had to school himself again right from the beginning. Even T. E. Lawrence might have envied such paramount *will*.

Alain Bombard was an incredible man and he remains "an image to the mighty world."

Alain Gerbault is another Frenchman in the North Atlantic who was neither a fame seeker nor a pothunter. He had no desire for money, easy or otherwise, and enhancing the glory of the flag was a preoccupation he was quite happy to leave in other hands; moreover, unlike Bombard, he didn't even have a theory to prove; he was there simply because he wanted to be at sea and alone.

Trained as a civil engineer, Gerbault fought in the air during the First World War and emerged from it physically unscathed but saddened by the loss of so many of his friends and unable to settle into the life for which he had been trained. Cutting loose from it all, he spent a year looking for a boat he could handle alone; and in 1921, after drawing a blank in France, he found his dream ship in England.

She was the *Firecrest*, a vessel built thirty years before at Rowhedge in Essex. Thirty-nine feet overall and thirty on the waterline, she was both narrow and deep for such a length, her maximum beam being eight feet six and her draft seven feet. She was ballasted with six and a half tons of lead — half of it on her keel and the rest stowed in her bottom. This made it practically impossible for her to capsize in any circumstances. Built of English oak and teak, it seemed that strength had been the overriding consideration in her design.

Consequently her flush deck was unbroken except for a single companionway, two skylights, a small hatch forward and another into the sail locker; and Gerbault boasted she was safe in any kind of sea. At that time single-handed sailors favored the ketch or the schooner, but the *Firecrest* was cutter-rigged. Gerbault called it a matter of taste. "Personally," he said, "I prefer to reef sails rather than take them in. In any case, I have found that the cutter is the best cruising rig for a small boat because it gives the maximum speed with the minimum sail area . . ."

Below decks, the *Firecrest* was divided into three compartments. The sleeping cabin was right aft. There was nothing primitive about it either. It had two bunks with lockers underneath, bookracks and a washbasin supplied from a fifteen-gallon tank under the deck; but the final touch was the paneling of mahogany and bird's-eye maple. The midships compartment was the saloon, also paneled in mahogany and bird's-eye maple and furnished with more bookracks, bringing the total aboard up to fourteen feet, which makes room for a lot of books. There was a table, of course, with cushioned lockers and various cupboards. Then forward was the galley, with a couple of folding cots for spare and a Swedish kerosene stove hung in gimbals. Here too were the freshwater pump and lockers for the stowage of provisions.

Having bought his boat, Gerbault loaded what he wanted into her and disposed of all the rest of his possessions, except his books. From then on the *Fire-*

crest was to be the only home he had or wanted, and what she carried, the total of all his worldly goods. He was cutting loose and property, apart from his boat and the means to keep her sailing, was already junk in his eyes. The only other thing he valued was his books. He had something like two hundred of them — "all books of adventure or poems . . ."

Significantly, his favorite poet was Masefield, his favorite authors Melville and Kipling, and he did not care much for Stevenson, who ". . . seems never to have been a sailor at heart . . . for he never described that which is beautiful about the life and hardships of sailors."

So Alain Gerbault dropped out and, after cruising around in the Mediterranean for a while, decided to try a trip across the Atlantic. "It was only for the fun of the thing," he says, "and to prove to myself that I could do it all alone . . ."

Leaving Cannes on April 27, he immediately ran into heavy weather. Running before the wind, first day out, he was logging ten knots and started carrying away gear. In that one blow, the rolling device on the gooseneck of the mainsail broke, a topping lift parted, and a jib halyard followed suit, though he saved the sail. After the storm came a spell of light airs which kept him backing and filling so long it was May 15 before he arrived at Gibraltar.

This was his point of departure. He planned to head westward on a great arc to a point south of Bermuda and thence head up for New York. The distance was approximately 4500 miles. At that time nobody had even attempted to sail the Atlantic from east to west alone, though Joshua Slocum on his famous trip around the world (of which more later), did it the other way in 1895. He called at the Azores and his greatest distance without landing was 2000 miles, his longest passage between ports, seventy-two days. Gerbault, guessing he would be out longer than that, stored for four months and on June 6, left Gibraltar "happy at the thought of the difficulties to be overcome."

He was in trouble from the very beginning, for his jib blew out of the bolt ropes before he had dropped the land astern. That set the pattern, and there wasn't a day passed which didn't bring some failure of sails, rigging, or gear to be made good. On July 8 — thirty-two days out — he records of the mainsail:

> . . . there was now not a single seam in it which I had not sewn together once and there were many that had been resown several times, almost clear across the breadth of the sail.

And that was only one thing. When he got down to examining his stores, he found the ship chandler had swindled him outrageously, especially in regard to his supply of salt beef which "was good on the top of the barrel but further down . . . largely made up of bones and fat." Then in 31 degrees west longitude, he discovered that most of his fresh water had spoiled. He had fifteen gallons of drinkable stuff left and 2500 miles still to go. From then on he rationed himself to "one small glass a day."

His biggest problem, however, was the fact that the *Firecrest* would not steer herself under anything like full sail, and for the first fourteen days or so, he had to heave her to whenever he needed to sleep. He got over this in the end by shortening down to a leg of mutton sail without a boom and the jib sheeted in flat. This reduced his speed so much that he gained no distance by keeping her going; but it gave him more rest and left him free for maintenance work and chores like cooking.

Like any sensible man living alone, he hammered the daily tasks down into a routine and performed them by the clock. This way they became almost part of his reflexes and made the minimum demands on his time, energy, and thought processes. So he turned out at five o'clock every morning to wash and cook breakfast. This never varied and consisted of oatmeal porridge, bacon, buttered ship's biscuits, and tea with condensed milk. At six he went up on deck, shook out the reefs and adjusted the sails as necessary, washed down, then got busy with the repairs and maintenance. Apart from a snack lunch at midday, he worked through till sundown, after which he cooked his main meal of salt beef, rice, and potatoes. This eaten and cleared away, he battened down for the night, turning in with his books by the light of a kerosene lamp hung in gimbals.

There were, of course, interruptions to the routine,

and moments of intense excitement, even danger. On
June 15, for example, the bobstay carried away and
to repair it, he had to cling with his legs to the bowsprit,
being dipped under completely several times before the
job was finished. On July 10, the wire steadying the
masthead when on the starboard tack parted, and he
had to shinny up the mast to replace it. On July 13,
when the spinnaker boom broke, he actually fell overboard trying to recover it and just saved himself by a
blind grab at the bobstay. The risk of making a false
step and going overboard was always there whenever
he moved about the deck; but he had no fear of death
or of pain, contemplating both with absolute equanimity
and the same interest that he bestowed on all natural
phenomena. Most people would have considered his
existence a boring one, flat and savorless as life in a
monastery — but not Gerbault. Around the end of
July he wrote:

> My conditions at this stage were anything but
> enviable. Rotten sails which required constant
> sewing and patching; a little bad water; fever
> and no wind. It gave no joyful feeling, but a
> certain sense of satisfaction in meeting and sur-
> mounting these obstacles . . .

At the beginning of August he dumped his cask
of salt beef, which was stinking, and then on the seventh
collected about ten gallons of rainwater in a tropical

storm. He also speared a bonito and felt that whatever else happened, he would not lack food or water. "I was therefore now quite contented, even happy," he wrote, "and in no hurry to get to New York."

On August 9 he was sixty-four days out and still 500 miles east of Bermuda, 1200 from New York, still fighting head winds, still mending his rotten sails and worn-out gear, and still on top of the world. On the tenth, after a particularly savage gale from the west, he squared up down below, going through everything he possessed and throwing overboard the items for which he had no immediate use. This was a periodic exercise which "always gives considerable pleasure, for it is one of the joys of the sea that you are not obliged to keep with you things you dislike."

So he and his boat struggled on. She was making water now, and on August 18 his pump broke down and it was impossible to get her even reasonably dry. Soon the cabin floor was awash and when the boat heeled to the wind, water surged into the bunks and lockers, spoiling everything. But Gerbault remained indomitable.

> Neither the baffling gales that ripped the sails and set the lockers awash, nor exposure to drenching seas and cutting rains were sufficient to burn the sea-fever out of my veins [he wrote]. I had a feeling, too, that there was a pretty good chance that some day the *Firecrest* and I would encounter a storm that we should not weather.

On August 20 the *Firecrest* emerged from an enormous sea with her bowsprit broken off short, the shrouds hanging loose, and the mast swaying dangerously. Gerbault made good the damage, mended the pump, got her dry, and put her back on her course. In that one day, he says: "I had been, in succession, yacht-hand, cook, rigger, carpenter, skipper, and navigator and, although absolutely done, was rather pleased with myself in consequence."

He ran out of potatoes next, and having lost his fish spear, was reduced to a diet of cereal, rice, and bacon; then on August 28 during the night he sighted a steamer passing westward with all her lights blazing. He was eighty-two days out and his only comment was: "Evidently the world of water was no more my own, and in consequence I felt a little sad . . ." Two days later he spoke a Greek emigrant ship bound for New York and had little joy of her. The crew treated him like something out of a freak show, and all they could think to give him was three bottles of brandy and some canned fish, neither of which he liked anyhow. "After this incident," he says, "the horizon was soon free again and I was pleased to be alone."

He had reached a state of mind now where deep down he didn't want the voyage to end; yet he wasn't so crazy as to imagine he could continue it indefinitely, and, pressing on, he sighted Nantucket Island on the morning of September 10, which made him ninety-four days from departure to landfall. He felt no elation, not even a sense of relief:

> On the contrary [he says], I felt a little sad, for
> I realised that it stood out there forecasting the
> end of my cruise . . . No longer would I be
> king of all I surveyed, but amongst human be-
> ings and a sharer in civilisation once more.

Even so, he still had a long way to go and it was not
till two o'clock in the morning of September 15 that
he dropped anchor off Fort Totten, after a final spell
of seventy-two hours at the tiller. The voyage of the
Firecrest was over, one hundred and one days after it
started from Gibraltar harbor.

There are many who would consider Alain Gerbault
foolhardy to embark on such an enterprise in the first
place, and mad to persist in it against such odds; but true
loners will admire him and envy him his experience; for,
as Maurice Hertzog says in his preface to Eric Tabarly's
Lonely Victory:

> . . . Mastery over oneself is perhaps the only
> mastery needed; everything follows from that.
> There-in lies courage — it is not madness but
> reasoned tenacity.

In the annals of small-boat sailing Gerbault's epic
voyage went down as a memorable first; but it was not
allowed to rest there merely as an achievement to be
admired. Before long, men being what they are, it had
become a challenge, a feat to be emulated and if possible
surpassed; and thus the element of competition got into
single-handed Atlantic sailing.

The idea of a race for solo yachtsmen, east to west across the North Atlantic Ocean, was the brain child of Lieutenant Colonel H. G. Hasler, R.M., and first conceived in 1955. He claimed his purpose was a serious one. Such a race, he believed, would not only be a test of the participator's skill and resource but would also influence fundamentally small-boat design and the development of self-steering gear. In the beginning he put up the idea to the Slocum Society of New York, but found insufficient support to justify further action. Then in 1959, *The Observer* newspaper became interested and finally agreed to give the project active support and to provide trophies. The rest followed. The Royal Western Yacht Club agreed to organize the race and control the start, and the Slocum Society undertook to supervise the finish.

The rules of the race could not have been simpler. The contenders had to start from Plymouth and finish at the Ambrose Lightship off New York, and what they did in between was up to them.

There were five entries, representing a wide range of craft. Francis Chichester's thirteen-ton cutter, *Gypsy Moth III*, was the biggest, Jean Lacombe's *Cap Horn* — twenty-one feet overall — the smallest. In between were Hasler's folk-boat *Jester*, Valentine Howells's sloop-rigged *Eira*, and David Lewis's sloop *Cardinal Virtue*, all twenty-five footers.

Gerbault's problem was simply to get there; but this group of pilgrims had to do it in the shortest possible time. This meant selecting the route offering, if not

a favorable wind which was against nature, then the
best chance of making headway under whatever conditions might prevail; and it would not necessarily be
the shortest way across. In the event, Hasler took the
high northern route, known to a generation of tramp-
steamer men as *north-about;* Chichester and Lewis took
the shortest Great Circle course, while Howells and
Lacombe opted for the long way around by the Azores.

The start was scheduled for June 11, 1960, and although Lacombe was delayed and started later, the
other four crossed the line at eleven o'clock that morning.

Given a boat and gear that would stand up to the
prolonged strain, there were two main hazards — the
danger of being run down in fog, and the possibility
of hitting an iceberg. It was Chichester's intention to
heave to and keep watch during fog, which he expected
to encounter over about 10 percent of the distance,
i.e., about 300 miles. When it came to the push, however, he sailed through 1430 miles of it and never
slowed down:

> It did not slow me down directly [he says], but
> indirectly it did, because sometimes I would lie
> in my bunk for hours before I got the necessary
> peace of mind to drop off to sleep. My reason
> told me the chance of being run down in the
> broad Atlantic was infinitesimally small, but my
> instinct said you must be a fool to believe that.

There was something uncanny about charging
at full speed through this dense impenetrable
fog, especially on a dark night.

In spite of a pretty rugged spell to begin with,
Chichester was first across the finish line. His time was
40 days 12 hours and 30 minutes and he sailed 4004½
miles to make good the distance of 3000 on the Great
Circle Course. Hasler, arriving eight days later, made
a poor second, while Lewis took 56 days, Howells 65,
and Lacombe 69.

Chichester must rank high on any list of men who
have dared to be *themselves alone* and do their own
thing, regardless. Even at Marlborough, where he received his formal education, he was considered to be
"too much of a rebel"; and looking back on that period
of his life, he wrote:

> There was something mean and niggardly about
> our existence at Marlborough; we seemed to be
> mentally, morally, and physically constipated.
> The whole emphasis was on what you must *not*
> do, and I consider that I am only now beginning
> to shake off the deeply rooted inhibitions which
> had gripped me by the time I left . . .

As a boy he cultivated solitude, spending whole days
roaming the Devonshire woods, "and it was part of
the fun never to be seen by anybody . . ." Later,
after emigrating to New Zealand, he learned to fly;

then with a solo flight from London to Australia and another from New Zealand to Australia to his credit, he set out for Tokyo, still finding that strange satisfaction in solitude. Putting down north of Brisbane, he writes: "There was no trace of man: alighting there was an indescribable thrill and the silence and solitude were a balm." But by the time he got to Manila he was hankering for a more lasting solitude than an aircraft could give him:

> Sometimes I day-dreamed of being alone on a yacht, lying on the deck and doing nothing but lazily sail it across the Pacific . . .

In flying it was the hurrying on that bothered him. ". . . one is no sooner aquainted with any place or person than one must leave them and fly on again," he wrote, and there seems always to have been a very sharp distinction in his mind between being *alone* and being *lonely*.

A crash in Japan put an end to his flight but, though he was very badly injured in the accident, he survived, to develop a passion for single-handed sailing. He felt he was cut out for it, never doing anything so well or enjoying anything so much when he was with other people. Writing of that first solo crossing he says:

> . . . I came to terms with life. I found that my sense of humour had returned; things which would have irritated me or maddened and in-furiated me ashore made me laugh out loud, and

I dealt with them steadily and efficiently. Rain, fog, gale, squalls and turbulent forceful seas under grey skies became merely obstacles. I seemed to have found the true values of life . . .

He took the troubles and trials, the discomforts and hardships, the frustrations and the dangers in his stride; the bad things never got him down and the good ones were all superlatives. Thus:

The meals I cooked myself were feasts, and my noggins of whisky were nectar. A good sleep was as valuable to me as the Koh-i-noor diamond. All my senses seemed to be sharpened; I perceived and enjoyed the changing character of the sea, the colours of the sky, the slightest change in the noises of the sea and wind, even the differences between light and darkness were strong, and a joy. I was enjoying life, and treating it as it should be treated — lightly.

On June 1, 1962, he set out from Plymouth on a second solo crossing and reached new peaks of fulfillment and happiness after another bad time at the beginning.

I was bursting with fitness and *joie de vivre*, that seemed to build up after a few weeks alone [he wrote afterward]. Perhaps it had taken three weeks to shed the materialism of ordinary living. I had become twice as efficient as when with people . . . I have never enjoyed anything more than that marvellous last 1000 miles sailing along the eastern seaboard of North America.

By 1964 the rules of the race had become more precise. There was still complete freedom of choice as to route; and the size and type of boat was also left to the fancy of the competitor, except that it had to be wind-driven and worked by the muscles of a one-man crew. That is to say, no mechanical power was allowed on board except to provide current for lighting and/or radio equipment. The acceptance of help or assistance in any shape or form during the crossing would automatically disqualify the entrant. Finally the finish was now Newport, Rhode Island, instead of the Ambrose Lightship, though the starting point was still Plymouth.

Almost predictably the 1964 event was won by a Frenchman, Eric Tabarly, in a boat specially designed and built for the job. She was the *Pen Duick II*, a ketch, 32 feet on the waterline and 44 feet overall; 11 feet maximum beam and drawing 7 feet of water. She was lightly built of plywood on a timber frame strengthened with metal ribs and steel plates. Her sail area was about 600 square feet.

The press had given the race an enormous build-up. Consequently the start was a mixture of regatta, carnival, and circus.

. . . the Sound was swarming with craft of all kinds and the Hoe and the beaches were dense

with spectators . . . this melee of sailing and
power boats, of graceful ocean racers, Navy
barges, launches and dinghies, all packed with
spectators and making in every direction . . .

It was even worse at the finish. Tabarly was inter-
viewed three times even before he crossed the line,
which he did hemmed in by press boats and besieged
by photographers with a host of small craft, tugboats,
fire-floats, and launches, tearing down on him, foghorns
and hooters blaring.

Yet it seems he got very little fun out of the trip.
He was completely dominated by the twin ideas of
speed and time; so much so that he had an alarm clock
set to wake him at ninety-minute intervals in order to
check the course and adjust the sails to maintain the
maximum speed. He had no time to read; no free time
at all, in fact, which is in marked contrast to Joshua
Slocum, who didn't give a tinker's curse about speed
because he wasn't racing anybody or trying to beat
anything and time didn't count. Jean Merrien sums
it up and Tabarly's experience seems to bear him out:

Yacht racing is to some extent contrary to the
spirit of the sea; in any case, that is not the kind
of sailing for pleasure which produces lone deep-
sea sailors.

III

Climbers on the Roof

Mountains have always inspired awe. In ancient times they were actually feared and generally avoided; but modern man, craving empty places in which to seek whatever it is he lacks, has accepted their challenge and learned to live with the awe. Today, mountaineering is described as a sport, but only for special people, and there is more in it for them than the kudos and the thrill of dangers survived and obstacles surmounted. George Leigh-Mallory, for example — to him it was a way of life, a spiritual necessity.

> . . . one feels that mountains had . . . transformed his scale of values and coloured his attitude to everything else. Mountaineering had become a religion . . . And it had, like other religions, its moments of ecstasy, of worship and of abasement . . .

And for Frank Smythe it was a recurring opportunity to see himself as he really was; it freed him from conventional attitudes and material values and gave him back "the simple and happy things of life."

As a sport, mountaineering dates only from around the middle of the nineteenth century, when it was developed by restless men cursed — or blessed, depending on the viewpoint — with an inability to accept the norm and find fulfillment in it. They needed to escape, physically and emotionally, from the restrictions and phony values of a society becoming increasingly affluent and ever more arid and sterile; so they lifted their eyes to the hills.

Until then mountains had seldom been climbed. Leonardo da Vinci in his day had a go at Monte Rosa on the Italian-Swiss border and made scientific observations from a snowfield on its slopes; in 1492 Mont Aiguille in the French Alps was scaled with ladders by the order and to the greater glory of King Charles VIII; and in 1786 a young French doctor named Paccard, accompanied by the guide, Jacques Balmat, got to the top of Mont Blanc. This started a minor craze for climbing, not mountains in general, but Mont Blanc in particular, and it lasted for over fifty years. Other peaks were being tackled during this period, but only occasionally, and under the guise of exploration or some scientific pursuit. Thus the Gross Glockner was scaled in 1800, the Ortler in 1804, the Jungfrau in 1811, the Finsteraarhorn in 1812, and the Wetterhorn in 1844. This last ascent, which was made from Grindelwald by Alfred Wills, is generally considered to mark the beginning of mountaineering as a sport.

The next decade saw most of the big peaks in the Alps being climbed, the last one to fall being the Matterhorn which, after many abortive attempts, was finally ascended by Edward Whymper in 1865.

Predictably mountaineers now sought other, still untrodden ranges — Freshfield went to Mount Elbrus (16,500 feet) in the Caucasus; Whymper to Ecuador for Chimborazo (20,700 feet) — and, in 1883, W. W. Graham went to Sikkim, where he reached 24,000 feet on Kabru. Thus man, doing his own thing, came to the Himalaya, sometimes called "the roof of the world," and he has been climbing there ever since.

The Himalaya in Central Asia is the highest and most extensive range of mountains in the world. The name is Sanskrit and means "Abode of Snow." It could not be more apt. The range has an overall length east and west of 1400 miles with a breadth north and south varying from 80 to 220 miles. It is best described as a series of roughly parallel ridges with the valleys between broken into a confusing maze by a multitude of subsidiary spurs. In its length there are no fewer than eighty-four peaks of over 24,000 feet, and it has an average height of 18,000 feet.

British, French, German, Swiss, American, Japanese — men of all nationalities have gone to the Himalaya and done big things. In 1931, the British, led by Frank Smythe, conquered Kamet (25,443 feet); in 1936 a combined English and American expedition got to the top of Nanda Devi (25,645 feet); in 1950 the French with Maurice Herzog put men on the summit of Annapurna (26,493 feet), the first peak over twenty-six thousand feet ever to be climbed; and since then, Nanga Parbat (26,620 feet), Cho Oyu (26,750 feet), Makalu (27,800 feet), Kangchenjunga (28,146), K2 (28,250 feet) have all fallen. So too has Everest (29,002 feet), highest in the world, first climbed in 1953 by Edmund Hillary, the New Zealand beekeeper, and Tensing Norkay, the Sherpa born near Makalu.

In the sixty-odd years between the first scramble to the summit of Mont Blanc and the conquest of Everest, mountaineering became, as well as a game, an art, with a vocabulary that is universal, recognizable styles, and a mystique that succeeding generations of practitioners have tried in vain to reveal to the uninitiated. The only way to learn why men go to the mountaintops is to start climbing. But there are techniques that can be acquired, and most of them come under the subheading of *rock climbing*. This, incidentally, has now developed into a separate sport, particularly in Great Britain, where sizable mountains are few and expensive to get at; so rock climbers can be found on any old cliff, crag, or rock face, so long as it presents problems. And skill on rock is an essential part of the mountaineer's equipment.

The really skilled operator can find holds on almost any rock face, no matter how sheer or smooth, just so long as there is some kind of a crack or fissure. Thus, writes J. F. Q. Barford in *Climbing in Britain*:

In a crack of the right width it is possible to in-
sert the fist and then clench it, so that the sides
of the hand are pressed firmly against the sides
of the crack. This is a most satisfactory hold
and the whole weight can quite confidently be
put on it, providing the crack is a suitable one.

This is called the *jammed fist* hold, and variations of the
same idea are the *jammed hand* and *jammed feet* holds.
Where the crack widens into a chimney, the climber
uses a method called *backing up*. Setting his back
against one wall, he gets his feet — or his knees, depending on the width of the fissure — against the other
and is thus jammed between the two. This is the resting position. When he is ready to move up, he presses
downward with one foot against the back wall and the
other against the front one, thus taking the weight off
his shoulders and allowing his body to lift to a slightly
higher position, the movement being repeated until the
top of the chimney is reached or some easier method
of progressing presents itself. Chimneys are really soft
options and the farther a climber is inside one, the more
secure he feels and is. Where there are adequate holds
in the back wall of the chimney, the climber uses a
variation of *backing up* called *straddling*, which utilizes
those holds, and is less strenuous and much faster. For
very narrow chimneys the method called *wriggling* —
a combination of body movements and hand pressures
— is used. Barford quotes as an example of this kind
of feature the Monolith Crack on the Gribin of Cwm

Idwal in North Wales. Where cracks are too narrow to jam into, they are climbed by a technique called a *layback*:

> Where the crack is in a corner, and with a sharp edge, you grip the edge, set your feet against the rock, and lift against your foot pressure. This is strenuous and calls for power because your arms are carrying more than your dead weight.

Given the techniques and the nerve to use them, the whole art of climbing is built on balance, which is achieved by keeping the body erect above the feet and letting them and the legs carry the weight and do most of the work. The hands and arms in the main are used as a safeguard and assurance of stability. Of course, situations that only a strong-arm effort can resolve do arise, but:

> By standing comfortably on the feet, or a single toe, and using the hands, or a finger, as retaining grips, you can keep your body balancing well clear of the rock; and so make sure of noticing all available holds and the best method and order of using them . . . This controlled and balanced progress from foothold to foothold is very economical of muscular energy, and it enables you to keep a reserve of strength in hand for the wrestles with awkward passages where your whole body may have to come into play.

From this it follows that muscular strength is not important in climbing, and that the worst possible mistake anybody can make on a mountain is to rush it. "Neatness," says Barford, "coolness, the settling before hand just what holds you will use and how, and then making the movement deliberately and smoothly, are what make the great climber."

The development of equipment for mountaineering has kept pace with the advances in techniques and the aspirations of climbers. In the beginning any old rope and an alpenstock, a pair of knickerbockers and an old tweed jacket were gear enough to see a man on to the top of Mont Blanc; but now, much to the disgust of the purist, the climber starts upward festooned with bits of hardware and other artificial aids. First of all he will have a number of *slings*, lengths of rope or line varying from 5 to 7 feet, which can be made into loops of any size merely by joining the ends with a square knot. These can be used in difficult situations as stirrups, and they often simplify the problem of belaying the rope. Next he will be carrying *pitons*, which are metal spikes with a ring in one end. These are used to provide an anchorage where no natural one exists, and some climbers will drive in a piton as a substitute for a nonexistent hold. Another item of hardware in his equipment will be *snaplinks*, which are called *Karabiners* in Germany and *mousquetons* in France, and consist of an oval steel ring with a spring-loaded hinged link in one side. If he expects to encounter ice, the climber will be carrying *crampons* — metal spikes strapped to the sole of the boot. And of course he will need a hammer of some kind for the pitons. On long climbs he will also be carrying some kind of a tent, a sleeping bag, and cooking apparatus, while his clothing will be specially designed to give the maximum of protection from the weather with the minimum weight and interference with his movements. Finally, on some rock climbs he will wear a crash helmet to protect his head from falling stones.

Since Edmund Hillary and Sherpa Tensing reached the summit of Everest in 1953, mountaineers have traveled far and wide in search of other peaks still unclimbed; but the Himalayas retain their pull and are still the ultimate challenge. The reason for this is easy to find. It lies in the size and nature of the massif. This range of mountains is unique both in extent and in elevation. It presents what seems to be an endless variety of problems and continues to lift men to ever higher levels of resourcefulness, endurance, and self-abnegation. In the past, climbers have gone to the Himalayas because, in the words of Frank Smythe, "Too much comfort, too much ease made them restless and dissatisfied. Life was not worth while unless it was tested." Basically it is for the same reason that they go today, though the objective may be a new route up Annapurna or an attack on Everest from the other side.

In the Himalayas, the climber is confronted with three major difficulties. First there is the altitude, and the consequent thinness of the atmosphere. At 18,000 feet the oxygen content is only half what it is at sea level and the climber is already breathing faster and moving more slowly; but the higher he gets, the slower he moves, until he is taking as many as ten breaths for every upward step, and his gain in height is reduced to something less than 300 feet an hour. And oxygen starvation has other bad effects besides this slowing down of the climber. It robs him of his appetite, makes it difficult to sleep, and causes him to lose weight and strength at an alarming rate. To be able to climb at all above 18,000 feet, a man must first become acclimatized — which means gradually getting his body used to working in the rarefied atmosphere. In recent times, however, this particular problem has to some extent been overcome by the use of oxygen in cylinders, again to the horror of the purists.

The second special difficulty is the weather, which is at once the decisive factor, and unpredictable. The upper slopes of the peaks are swept by sudden blizzards; as much as six feet of fresh snow has been known to fall on Kangchenjunga in 48 hours; and air temperatures can without warning drop quickly to under 20 degrees below zero Fahrenheit. The experience of Herzog and Lachenal on Annapurna in 1950 illustrates the point. Camp V was established at 24,600 feet on the day before the final assault. By that time the operation had become a race against the monsoon, but the day had started fine enough, though it was very cold. The tent was pitched precariously on a platform hacked out of a snowfield sloping at 40 degrees, then anchored with two pitons driven into cracks in an outcropping rock-rib. The two men anticipated a grim night and got it. By nightfall a gale had sprung up, so fierce in the gusts that both men had to cling to the poles to prevent the tent from being blown away. The noise alone was intimidating in its immensity. "The air," says Herzog, "was fraught with terror, and in the end we became terrified too." Then suddenly it was snowing so heavily that the tent began to sag under the weight of it, threatening to suffocate the two men where they lay.

> I could no longer breathe [writes Herzog]. The weight of the snow was literally crushing me. Like a boxer on his guard, I held both arms to my chest and so made a small space which allowed me to expand my lungs. The noise of the wind was ear-splitting, and every onslaught was accompanied by a high-pitched whistling. The tent poles bent over dangerously, while with the strength of desperation we tried to hold them in place . . . We were worn out and utterly weary, but the storm saw to it that we were kept wide awake.

On the summit they were in the clear, with clouds far below them; but on the way back to Camp V, the weather changed again, the sky becoming completely covered with cloud and everything turning "grey and dirty-looking." A freezing wind sprang up, increasing in strength minute by minute, and they groped their way back to the tent through a thickening mist. Both men suffered severely from frostbite.

The third special difficulty, and perhaps the greatest danger, is the avalanche. There are places in the Himalayas where snow has been accumulating through the storms of centuries and has finally packed down into glaciers hundreds of feet thick. These huge masses are constantly but imperceptibly moving downward under the pull of gravity. Reaching the edge of a precipice, they project beyond it to form *hanging glaciers* such as those which are a notable feature of the northwest face of Kangchenjunga. From time to time the unsupported portion breaks away. "The resulting avalanches," says Smythe, "may weigh tens of thousands of tons, and in size may be a quarter of a mile in length and hundreds of feet in thickness." It is difficult to imagine the scale of these icefalls; even the wind they raise in passing is strong enough to flick a man off the face of the earth and whole parties have been wiped out by them. In 1937, for instance, a German expedition on Nanga Parbat, camping in what was thought to be absolute safety, was swept away in the night and sixteen of them killed. Of Kangchenjunga, Smythe writes:

> There is probably no mountain-side in the world which sends down greater avalanches than the northwest face of Kanchenjunga, for ice walls

miles in length and hundreds of feet in thickness defend the mountain from attack and cast loose avalanche after avalanche on to the glaciers beneath, and woe betide any one who comes within range of this natural artillery.

This Frank Smythe was a great one for the high lonely places. He climbed in the Alps and the Rockies as well as in the Himalayas, where he made a bold bid for the top of Kangchenjunga. The attempt failed, but in 1931 he became the first man ever to stand on the summit of Kamet (25,443 feet). He subsequently played a big part in three Everest expeditions. He loved mountains and wrote of them superlatively. Of the prospect from the summit of Kamet, for instance, he said:

What I remember best was the isolation and silence, we felt ourselves to be far removed from the world and poised as it were in space. I remember also a multitude of mountains and clouds, mountains of rock and ice and snow, grand and immovable, between which huge clouds rose slowly, apparently as solid as the mountains themselves. I remember an atmosphere of unearthly brilliance in which ranges two hundred or more miles away showed perfectly sharp and clear-cut, among them some mountains that can only have been the Karakoram Himalaya nearly three hundred miles distant, whilst to the north we gazed across the honey-coloured plains of Tibet, on which small white clouds moved like yachts, stretching illimitably into Central Asia. Over this tremendous scene of mountain, valley, plain and cloud, the sun poured its radiance from a sky of dark sapphire blue, a blue so profound that seated on the summit of Kamet we could sense the limitless abysses of space . . .

The three special difficulties described constitute the main defenses of the big Himalayan peaks. On Kang-chenjunga it is *avalanches* and *ice walls*, on Annapurna, steep *snow and ice slopes* and *precipitous rock pitches*, and on Everest, *altitude* and *weather*, both of which seem relatively easy but proved to be the hardest to beat. In all, eleven expeditions were mounted against Everest before it fell and the siege lasted thirty years. Even then it was oxygen that swung the balance.

Everest, or Chomolunga ("Goddess Mother of the World" in Tibetan) stands on the frontier between eastern Nepal and Tibet. The figure of 29,002 feet generally accepted as its height, is the mean of six cal-culations made in 1852. It is named after Sir George Everest, at one time a surveyor general in India.

The attacks on the mountain were as follows:

1. *1921:* A reconnaissance, sent out from Britain by the Alpine Club and the Royal Geographical Society. The approach was made through Tibet and, surveying the approaches from that side, the party discovered a possible route up the north ridge.

2. *1922:* Following the route suggested by the 1921 expedition, one climbing party reached 26,700 feet without oxygen and another 27,300 with it.

3. *1924:* This turned out to be an abnormally bad weather year with terrible snowstorms. Nevertheless, Norton and Somervell together got to 28,000 feet without oxygen and Somervell went on alone to 28,130 feet. Then George Leigh-Mallory and Irvine tried for the top with oxygen. They were seen climbing at about 28,000 feet when they disappeared, and their bodies were never recovered.

4. *1933:* Still using the north ridge, Frank Smythe, Wyn Harris, and Wager reached 28,100 feet without oxygen and found Mallory's ice axe.

5. *1935*
6. *1936* These three attempts were even less successful than previous ones.
7. *1938*

8. *1951:* A British expedition through Nepal reconnoitered a completely new route, leading up to the south face by way of the Khombu Glacier.

9, 10. *1952:* Two Swiss expeditions, one of which put Raymond Lambert and Sherpa Tensing Norkay 28,200 feet up on the southeast ridge.

11. *1953:* A British expedition under Sir John Hunt put two men, using oxygen, on the summit on May 29.

So the ultimate triumph in high places belongs to Hillary and the Sherpa Tensing; but, rather than these two, it is for Mallory that the mountain stands as a monument.

George Leigh-Mallory was born on June 18, 1886,

which made him thirty-nine years old when he started up Everest for the last time. As a boy he already had a passion for climbing, which he indulged on anything available — walls, roofs, trees, what have you — demonstrating a natural sense of balance that matched his remarkable disregard for personal danger. He was by no means foolhardy but, always aware of the risks involved in the things he did, he really enjoyed taking them; or, as his biographer, David Pye, puts it, he liked "doing things with a small margin of safety." So all through his life he preferred to catch a train with five seconds in hand rather than five minutes, and he was forever on the lookout for corners to cut, time to save, and space to conserve.

In 1910, after the usual formal education at Winchester and Magdalene College, Cambridge he became a schoolmaster at Charterhouse, but long before that he was climbing in the Alps, and had been recognized as an outstanding mountaineer. The game, as he saw it, called for:

> . . . the exercise of moral qualities, patience, and self-control, and sometimes fortitude, and the subordination of all else to the striving towards an end greater than himself.

During the 1914–1918 war, he served as a subaltern in artillery, and during this period he was forced for long spells into close contact with numbers of people who shared neither his ideas nor his values. The experience taught him sympathy and tolerance, but he found it unpleasant.

> I'm sure there never was such a lover of his own company as I am [he wrote]. I hope I have learnt how to suffer an excess of companions in a confined space, but I can never forgive or forget the excess of time that passes away with no addition to one's store of amusing thoughts.

Reading his correspondence, David Pye got ". . . a strong sense of his carrying on a life apart, a life of conscious thought and self-examination, through all the monotony . . ."

When the time came to select the team for the 1921 expedition to Everest, Mallory was a natural choice. He played a leading part in the reconnaissance, and when the expedition turned homeward he was hooked on the mountain. In 1922 he was back again, he being the character who got to 26,700 feet without oxygen that year. Then came the 1924 bid, and by that time the climbing of Everest had become an obsession to him. "For weeks and months," says Pye, "his whole mind had been concentrated on the evolution of plans in their remotest detail, and his body in carrying them out."

Accompanied by Irvine, Mallory spent the night of June 7 at Camp VI (26,800 feet), leaving N. E. Odell at Camp V (25,300 feet). The weather was most promising then and the outlook magnificent almost beyond belief.

To the westward [writes Odell] was a savagely wild jumble of peaks towering above the upper Rongbuk Glacier and its many affluents, culminating in the mighty Cho-uyo (26,750 feet) and Gyachung Kang (25,910 feet) bathed in pinks and yellows of the most exquisite tints. Right opposite were the gaunt cliffs of Everest's North Peak, their banded structure pregnant with more special and esoteric interest of their past primeval history and in this respect not detracting by its impression from the vision of such as can behold with more than single eye. This massive pyramid of rock, the one near thing on God's earth, seemed only to lend greater distance to the wide horizon which it intercepted, and its dark bulk the more exaggerate the brilliant opalescence of the far northern horizon of Central Tibet, above which the sharp-cut crests of distant peaks thrust their purple fangs, one in particular rising supreme among them. To the eastward, floating in thin air, 100 miles away, the snowy top of Kangchenjunga appeared, and nearer, the beautifully varied outline of the Gyankar Range, that guards the tortuous passages of the Arun in its headlong plunge towards the lowlands of Nepal. It has been my good fortune to climb many peaks alone and witness sunset from not a few, but this was the crowning experience of them all, an ineffable transcendent experience that can never fade from the memory.

Leaving Camp V on the morning of the eighth, Odell climbed about 700 feet and from the top of a small crag, looked upward. Then, he says,

> . . . there was a sudden clearing of the atmosphere above me and I saw the whole summit ridge and final peak of Everest unveiled. I noticed far away on a snow slope leading up to what seemed to me to be the last step but one from the base of the final pyramid, a tiny object moving and approaching the rock step. A second object followed, and then the first climbed to the top of the step. As I stood intently watching this dramatic appearance, the scene became enveloped in cloud once more, and I could not actually be certain that I saw the second figure join the first.

It is estimated they were then 800 feet below the summit and Odell reckoned they were going well; but it was 12:50 P.M. and they were a long way behind their schedule. They were never seen again. Odell, who, in his quiet way, sticks in the memory as a man bigger than life, waited for them through the day and next morning climbed up to Camp VI but found no trace of them. So how, when, and precisely where they died no one knows. Only the questions remain.

Did they reach the summit and run out of steam on the way down? Did one of them slip fatally and drag the other off the rock with him? Were they so late that darkness caught them before they could get back to the shelter of Camp VI? And so on.

Norton, the leader of the expedition, said afterward that it was impossible to tell whether Mallory was a tired man or not. He might well have been and failed to realize the fact; it might well have been that his passion for the mountain drove him on even when the last dregs of his strength were gone. If this were so and they did reach the top, then it might have been that exhaustion caught up with him in the moment of triumph and he went out like a light. "This for one, would mean the end for both . . ." says David Pye. It is all speculation but something like this must have been in Odell's mind when he looked up at the mountain before leaving Camp VI for the last time:

> . . . as I gazed again [he wrote], another mood appeared to creep over her haunting features. There seemed to be something alluring in that towering presence. I was almost fascinated. I realised that no mere mountaineer alone could but be fascinated, that he who approaches close must ever be led on, and oblivious of all obstacles seek to reach that most sacred and highest place of all . . .

The disappearance of Mallory and Irvine seems to have been the high point of the struggle for Everest, though it went on for almost thirty more years. It is as if these two by dying on it had both proved the mountain and appeased it. What remained to be done was in a sense consolidation; but to say that those who did it knew more and were better equipped for the task because of Mallory and Irvine in no way detracts from their achievement.

In 1933, Frank Smythe got within 1000 feet of the summit. He spent the night alone at their Camp VI, which had been established at 27,400 feet; but when he set out in the morning, he was accompanied by Eric Shipton, who presently became unwell and returned, leaving Smythe to go on alone in an attempt to reach the top. The climbing, he says, was not difficult to begin with, though a slip would have sent him hurtling down to destruction. At about 28,000 feet he was on a band of yellow rock, along the top of which he had to traverse horizontally to a great gully that cut into the north face of the mountain. Then, after crossing the gully he would have to climb about 400 feet up a steep rock-buttress onto the final pyramid. The traverse was complicated by two intervening beds of frozen snow, across which it was necessary to cut steps. This was at that height an incredibly exhausting task which slowed him considerably and burned up much more energy than he could afford to spend at that stage. Nevertheless he gained the gully; but as he did so, his buoyant optimism died and was replaced by a feeling of despair, for the last buttress was covered to a depth of up to three feet with freshly fallen snow, while the gully itself was choked with the stuff, wind-blown and hard. It was lying at an angle of about 50 degrees and to cross it meant more step-cutting. Something inside forced him on. He cut the steps — about twenty of them — and at last stood under the final buttress, where one look told him that the soft, powdery snow covering the rock made the summit inaccessible that day. It was the worst kind of snow, and everything he knew about mountaineering told him he was beaten as soon as he encountered it; but he still went on. For a whole hour he went on, making a net gain in height of fifty feet, and burning himself up in the process; and at that point he realized he was in grave danger of being caught on the mountain at nightfall and decided to turn back. It was then he knew the ultimate loneliness.

> I was alone [he wrote]. There was no sign of my companion. I seemed engulfed in a profound and awful silence. I trod the very boundaries of life and death on the topmost pinnacle of the earth's surface . . .

He made it back, of course, rejoining Shipton at Camp VI, who presently took himself off to Camp V so Smythe might have a more comfortable night in the tiny tent. Just before Smythe settled down for the long twelve hours of darkness, he looked outside.

> It was [he says] a scene of incredible desolation.
> All round were great slabs of rocks mortared

with snow in their interstices like an immense
expanse of armour plating. Thousands of feet
beneath lay a great sea of cloud slowly writhing
and twisting in its uppermost billows and here
and there seeming almost on fire, where it was
touched by the rays of the setting sun. There was
not a sound. No stonefall or avalanche disturbed
the serenity of Everest. There was silence, an
absolute and complete silence; and permeating
all, investing all, with a deadly embrace, was the
cold, the coldness that reigns in the abysses of
space.

The weather broke that night; Smythe dropped down
to Camp IV in a blizzard next morning, and the 1933
attempt on Everest was over.

It might be fitting to finish up with another quotation
from Frank Smythe, for the rest of the Everest story
is recent history and has little to do with men alone as
such, for:

> . . . If everything we do in life is to be measured
> in terms of money [he wrote], then life would
> be a very poor thing . . . In mountaineering,
> and on Mount Everest in particular, a man sees
> himself for what he is. He learns the value of
> comradeship and of service . . . he sees life for
> the grand thing it is . . . The cares of civilisa-
> tion slip away. Seen from the snows of the Him-
> alayas, war and the threat of war, the jumble and
> hurly-burly of speed, noise and rush, the anxie-

ties and uncertainties of this maelstrom we call
"civilisation," appear for what they are worth.
Life becomes simple and simplicity is the soul-
mate of happiness . . .

Smythe didn't see the finish; he died in 1949 still
on the sunny side of his half century.

IV

The Gypsies of the Horn

On the map of the world there are three names with a very special significance for seafaring men, haunting alike the memories of those who knew the sailing-ship era and the dreams of enthusiastic amateur sailors hooked on single-handed navigation. They are the Cape of Good Hope at the southern tip of Africa, Cape Leeuwin on the southwestern corner of Australia, and Cape Horn, southernmost point of South America. All three of them have a pretty grim reputation as to weather. Nobody knows how many fine ships and honest, hard-working sailormen have been lost in their vicinity; but if a prize were offered for the highest score in this respect, Cape Horn would win it by a large margin.

The Horn is a headland on a small island — Horn Island — in the Fuegian Archipelago. Lying in about the fifty-sixth parallel of south latitude, it is a bleak, barren place. Magellan never got that far south, passing from the Atlantic to the Pacific by the narrow tortuous channel that bears his name and separates the big island of Tierra del Fuego from the main mass of the American continent. Following him in 1578, Sir Francis Drake should also have missed it, but after getting through the narrows into the Pacific, he was driven by wild weather, first to the southward and then to the eastward until he was in the Atlantic again; and as he fought his way back to the westward, he glimpsed the headland through the murk. Consequently that stretch of wild water lying between Cape Horn and the northern edge of Antarctica is called Drake Strait. It was nearly forty years after that, in 1616, that two Dutchmen, La Maire and Van Schouten, identified the place for what it was and named it after their home town of Hoorn.

Today the boundary between the Argentine and Chile lies to the east of Horn Island, which therefore comes under the jurisdiction of the latter. It boasts a lighthouse, 128 feet high, the characteristic of which, according to the Admiralty chart of the area, is a flash every ten seconds with a maximum visibility of eleven miles. Other place names in the area often bandied about by seafarers are Staten Island to the northeast and Diego Ramirez to the southwest.

In the pretechnological age — that wonderful time of "wooden ships and iron men" — old salts were inclined to credit the Horn with sentience and personality. Such hostility to ships and sailormen, such implacable cruelty as they continually experienced there were against nature, they argued. Storms they could understand and accept; hurricanes, typhoons, huge seas, blistering heat, and freezing cold were occupational hazards and in their own phrase, they signed on chancing them; but there was no gamble about what happened around the Horn. It was a sure thing. The place was evil; it had it in for them and whatever the rest of the voyage might bring, there they would find only suffering and heartbreak, torment and soul-killing labor till they either won clear of its clutches or were swept to oblivion in its shadow.

This, of course, was pure superstition. The Horn has no soul, evil or otherwise, and the wild weather that rages in the vicinity is caused by objective factors that can be identified with certainty and even measured with some degree of accuracy. In the weather pattern of the Southern Hemisphere there is a belt of almost constant westerly winds which stretches from about forty degrees south latitude to the edge of the Antarctic ice. The area is known to mariners by the self-explanatory term, *Roaring Forties*; and passing south of the Cape of Good Hope and south of Australia, it reaches right around the world. There is only one place where the free passage of these westerlies is challenged and that is the Drake Strait, the bottleneck five hundred or so miles wide formed by the tip of South America reaching down toward the icebound peninsula of Graham Land thrusting northward out of Antarctica. Hence the ferocity of the winds and the enormity of the seas in this vicinity.

For a long time after Magellan and Drake, the passage around the Horn was little used. George Anson went that way on his circumnavigation; so did James Cook in search of the Great South Land; and there were the buccaneers like William Dampier after the Spanish treasure ships heading for the Isthmus of Panama from the Philippines and the coasts of Chile and Peru. The route became a little busier around the beginning of the nineteenth century, when the Americans started to get in on the China trade, but it was still a rather lonely place even in 1832 when Richard Dana made his famous voyage from Boston to California.

Dana sailed as a foremast hand aboard the brig *Pilgrim* and was one hundred and fifty days on passage. Approaching the Horn, the signs were good and the crew had hopes of getting around the cape into the Pacific without too much anguish; but on Wednesday, November 5, they ran into a westerly gale, accompanied by sleet and hail, and with the decks waist deep in green water were forced to heave to. The night was wild, with rain, hail, and snow and the sea running very high; but the weather eased a bit next day and the *Pilgrim* was able to get back on her course to the westward. On the night of the sixth, however, the conditions worsened again. This time she shortened down to close-reefed topsails, balance-reefed trysail, and foretopmast staysail and went on trying to beat to windward. By daybreak on the seventh the wind had died completely and the brig was rolling heavily in a flat calm and dense fog; but it came on to blow again in the evening with more snow and hail. The *Pilgrim* was awash with green seas breaking over the bows, but the master kept her to it through the night, which was followed by another day of calm and thick fog, giving way to a gale-force wind with heavy snow at sundown. November 9 began fine and clear and remained that way until between 5:00 and 6:00 P.M., when once more the cry for *all hands* went up.

> A true specimen of Cape Horn was coming upon us. A great cloud of a dark slate-colour was driving on us from the south-west; and we did our best to take in sail . . . before we were in the midst of it. We had got the light sails furled, the courses hauled up, and the topsail reef-tackles hauled out, and were just mounting the fore-rigging when the storm struck us. In an instant the sea, which had been comparatively quiet, was running higher and higher; and it became almost as dark as night. The hail and sleet were harder than I had yet felt them; seeming to pin us down to the rigging. We were longer taking in sail than ever before; for the sails were stiff and wet, the ropes and rigging covered with snow and sleet, and we ourselves cold and nearly blinded with the violence of the storm. By the time we had got down upon deck again, the little brig was plunging madly into a tremendous head sea, which at every dive rushed in through the bow-ports and over the bows, and buried all the forward part of the vessel.

The *Pilgrim* never saw the end of that storm; but she kept on through it, clawing her way to windward and when, on the evening of November 14, she turned northward for Juan Fernández, it was still blowing.

Wild as it was, however, that was a relatively easy and quick passage the wrong way around — i.e., against the prevailing westerlies. There are cases on record of ships driven back so often that the master, despairing of ever reaching the west coast that way, has in the end gone about and run right around the world eastward to come at it across the Pacific.

Dana's return passage took only one hundred and thirty-seven days, but he had a harder time rounding the Horn. He had changed ships in California and was now a foremast hand aboard the *Alert*, which was bigger and better built than the old brig. She sailed from San Diego with a cargo of raw hides on May 8 and running to the southward found herself on June 26 in 47°50′ south latitude 113°40′ west longitude, with Cape Horn bearing east southeast, ½ east and 1800 miles away. The wind was then westerly and gale force, and they were all set for a storming run to the eastward and a quick turn northward for home. But it didn't work out that way. On July 2, when she was in the latitude of the Horn and about 21 degrees of longitude to the west of it, she ran into ice and the wind suddenly hauled south.

The berg alongside which they found themselves was a monster, and Dana's description of it is worth quoting, for the way it puts this particular hazard of the Horn into perspective:

> And there lay, floating in the ocean, several miles off, an immense irregular mass, its top and points covered with snow, and its centre of a deep indigo colour . . . As far as the eye could reach, the sea in every direction was of a deep blue colour, the waves running high and fresh, and sparkling in the light and in the midst lay this immense mountain island, its cavities and valleys thrown into deep shade, and its points and pinnacles glittering in the sun . . . no description can give any idea of the strangeness, splendour, and really, the sublimity, of the sight. Its great size — for it must have been from two to three miles in circumference, and several hundred feet in height — its slow motion, as its base rose and sank in the water, and its high points nodded against the clouds; the dashing of the waves upon it, which breaking high with foam, lined its base with a white crust; and the thundering sound of the cracking of the mass, and the breaking and tumbling down of huge pieces; together with its nearness and approach, which added a slight element of fear — all combined to give to it the character of true sublimity.

Two days later, she had made a fair bit of easting but set a long way to the northward in the process and she was still in ice. Between 9:00 A.M. and 3:00 P.M. —

the hours of daylight, that is — they saw thirty-four bergs of various sizes. Meanwhile the wind had become due east and increased to gale force with hail, sleet, and snow, to which was presently added thick fog. A long period followed in which head winds accompanied by snow or heavy rain alternated with fair winds and fog. So even when the wind was favorable, the bad visibility and the presence of ice made it impossible to run. In the end the master felt he had to get out of the ice somehow for the ship was sheathed in it, her rigging and sails so encased as to be almost unworkable. He headed her north northeast for Cape Pilar, determined to let the Horn have the best of the encounter and go through the Straits of Magellan instead.

By July 10 she was clear of the ice in 54°10′ south 79°07′ west and going fine; but on the eleventh the wind shifted again, coming away at gale force out of the east, accompanied by thick fog. The signs were that these conditions would persist, and that put an end to the idea of the Straits as a soft option. They "braced up on the larboard tack, put the ship's head due south and stuck her off for Cape Horn again." The visibility improved somewhat but remained poor, and she was soon back in among the ice with the wind still easterly; so presently she put about and ran northeast on a 200-mile leg that brought her dangerously near to the west coast of Tierra del Fuego. Again she went to the southward and for a brief spell actually got a westerly wind; but it didn't last, giving way to easterly gales that blew continuously for eight heartbreaking days. They kept with it, however, clawing to the eastward, and when it shifted south again they were at last in a position to use it. She finally cleared Staten Island and headed north into the Atlantic on July 22.

Dana's experience underlines two things about the Horn. One is the fact that, though the prevailing winds are westerly, a ship going either way might encounter a spell of head winds lasting for weeks. This is undoubtedly responsible in some part for the reputation the Cape holds for perversity, malice, and even murderous intent towards seafarers. The other point of interest that emerges is the extreme loneliness of the place. Outward bound, Dana saw only one other vessel in the five-month-long passage — the whaler *New England*, of Poughkeepsie, one hundred and twenty days out from New York and bound nowhere in particular. Homeward in the *Alert*, he saw none at all.

The discovery of gold in California in 1848 changed all that, at least for a while. In the two years that followed, 760 ships sailed round the Horn from American east coast ports alone. They carried between them 27,367 passengers, and more fortunes were made transporting people to the diggings and servicing them there than ever came out of the hopeful claims they staked. On top of all this, large-scale emigration to Australia was now under way and, though the outward route of the emigrant ships was eastward via the Cape of Good Hope, they all came back home round the Horn. This was the *golden age* of sail, and it built up steadily through the next forty years. The peak was reached just before the turn of the century, and in 1895 one shipmaster on passage to a west coast port estimated he had between 30 and 40 ships in sight at once off the Horn. They included Australian wool clippers, big wooden grain and timber ships from San Francisco and Puget Sound, Yankee clippers deep with case oil out of Philadelphia for Japan, English barques with Welsh coal to Valparaiso or homeward bound with phosphates and guano from Chile and Peru. It is impossible now to imagine the sight, because it didn't last. The sailing ship was already on the way out and the Panama Canal, along with a few other less obvious things, killed it stone dead. By 1920, the Horn was again numbered among the world's empty places. It remains a lure and a challenge to loners and other oddballs who don't know when they are well-off.

Famous among the loners is Captain Joshua Slocum. He was born in Nova Scotia on the shores of the Bay of Fundy on February 20, 1844. Thus he qualifies for the title of *bluenose*, given to seamen from this area, which is a great thing for a seafaring man to have, though he always called himself "a naturalized Yankee" and a citizen of the United States. His father was a farmer, but he had seafaring people on both sides of the family and he was tinkering with boats at the age of eight. He made his first voyage proper in the galley of a fishing schooner; but he was a bad cook and soon found himself sailing before the mast in a foreign-going, full-rigged ship. Eventually he came to command, and among the ships he sailed with distinction was the *Northern Light*, which he believed was "the finest American sailing vessel afloat." He was part owner of her, which might account for some of his enthusiasm. This was in the 1880s. Later he acquired and sailed the barque *Aquidneck*, which he finally left a total loss on the coast of Brazil. She was both his home and his lot and though he was able to build a kind of big canoe out of the wreckage and sail his family home to New York in it, he arrived flat broke.

Times were bad then for windjammers, and he made up his mind to quit the sea; but, as he said, "What was there for an old sailor to do?" A whaling captain of his acquaintance supplied him with the answer and the means in the shape of a dilapidated wreck of a sloop called the *Spray*, which was lying in the middle of a field at Fairhaven, near New Bedford. She had been there as a pain in the neck to her owner for seven long years, and he gave her to Slocum with his blessing.

It seemed a bit like a rather cruel joke, but Slocum didn't see it that way. Instead, he decided to rebuild the old wreck with his own hands; and this he did, even to the point of felling the timber and building a steam box in which to shape it.

> The bulwarks [he writes] I built up of white-oak stanchions, fourteen inches high and covered with seven-eighth inch white pine. These stanchions mortised through a two-inch covering board, I calked with thin cedar wedges. They have remained perfectly tight ever since. The deck I

made of one and a half inche by three inche white pine spiked to beams, six by six inches, of yellow or Georgia pine, placed three feet apart. The deck inclosures were one over the aperture of the main hatch, six feet by six for a cooking galley, and a trunk farther aft, about ten feet by twelve for a cabin. Both of these rose about three feet above the deck and were sunk sufficiently into the hold to afford head-room. In the spaces along the sides of the cabin, under the deck, I arranged a berth to sleep in and shelves for small storage, not forgetting a place for the medicine chest. In the midship hold, that is the space between cabin and galley under the deck was room for provision of water, salt beef, etc., ample for many months . . .

He gives the following dimensions for the *Spray*:

Length overall	36 feet 9 inches
Beam	14 feet 2 inches
Depth in the hold	4 feet 2 inches
Net tonnage	9 tons
Gross tonnage	12.71 tons

The thing that worried his friends was not how she would sail or whether she would float, but simply whether she would pay. This was the very last thing on Slocum's mind. He built her for fun. All he wanted out of her was the sheer joy of creating something with his hands out of his own mind, and he couldn't have cared less about the economics of it. In point of fact she cost 553 dollars and 62 cents for materials and thirteen months of his own labor, during which time he maintained himself by doing odd jobs on the whale ships that came into port to refit.

Such then was the famous *Spray* in which, by devious ways, Joshua Slocum, fifty-one years old and single-handed, came to the vicinity of the Horn. He had no illusions about what he was letting himself in for, even though he planned to avoid the worst of it by using the Straits. In the seven months since his departure from the New England coast, he had learned a lot about his boat and modified her considerably. At Rio de Janeiro, for instance, he had changed her from a sloop to a yawl, and in Buenos Aires he shortened her mainmast by seven feet and chopped five feet off the bowsprit, all with an eye to what lay ahead and the object of making her easier to handle.

It was February 11, 1896, when he rounded Cape Virgins into the Straits of Magellan, and the first part of the voyage was so easy he had arrived at Punta Arenas three days later. He was treated with great kindness there and on the nineteenth sailed for Cape Pilar and the Pacific, laden with gifts and stuffed to the ears with good advice. Again it looked easy, so long as he kept going and didn't get his throat cut by the savage Fuegians; but he had already run out of luck and it was not until April 13 that he finally cleared the Island of Tierra del Fuego and stood away for Juan Fernández. In the fifty-four days between, he experienced more than enough action, hardship, danger, and frustration to satisfy any ten ordinary men for the whole of their lives.

Head winds and blinding snow flurries were the least of his troubles; the biggest strain was the constant threat of violence from groups of savages stalking him in dugout canoes. By day he held them off with a little judicious rifle fire and by night strewed the deck with carpet tacks to discourage any attempt to board. He ran the *Spray* aground and got her off again. He filled his hold with tallow salvaged from a wrecked sailing ship. He reached Cape Pilar and entered the Pacific, only to be immediately caught in a wild storm that drove him southeast toward the Horn. When the weather permitted, he groped his way back into the Straits by way of the Cockburn Channel and sighted Punta Arenas for the second time, but pushed on. An American ship gave him much-needed food. "It was a glorious outfit of provisions of all kinds I got," he wrote. Again he had to put in for repairs, this time at Port Angosto. There he found the Argentine cruiser *Azopardo* at anchor and was boarded by her commander, who tried all ways to persuade him to abandon the voyage, offering to tow him to Punta Arenas if he would do so. Slocum resisted the blandishments and, declining the offer, pushed off again. This time he made it, and one can only imagine how light his heart must have been when at last he headed his ship northward toward the sun.

Slocum's voyage demonstrated as nothing else could have done the enormous range of the small, strongly built sailing boat, well-built and skillfully handled; and quite a number of such craft have dared the Roaring Forties in the vicinity of the Horn since his day. In January 1911, George Blyth and Peter Arapakis in the *Pandora*, sailing from Australia via the Pitcairn and Easter islands to New York, rounded the Cape, going with the prevailing winds. They had a rough passage, which reached its climax off Staten Island when she overturned in a violent squall and lost her mast. She was sighted by a whaling ship next day and towed into the Falkland Islands for repairs and eventually reached New York; but her number was up, for she sailed for Europe and was never heard of again.

The next one down there, also going from the Pacific into the Atlantic, was a 42-foot gaff cutter called *Saoirse* in which a Dublin man, Conor O'Brien, with a crew of three, sailed around the world in 1925–1927. Then in 1934 a character called Hansen sailed the 36-foot cutter *Mary Jane* from Río de la Plata to Ancud in Chile in the depth of the Southern Atlantic Ocean winter. It cost him 100 days and all the luck he had, for shortly after she was lost on the Chilean coast and he went with her. In 1942 an Argentinian single-hander, Vito Dumas, on a voyage around the world, running before the westerlies, made a storming passage of the Drake Strait on his way to Buenos Aires, setting records that were to stand for over twenty years. Another loner in the area was Marcel Bardiaux, who decided — and it would be futile to ask why — to go on a cruise among the islands of Tierra del Fuego in midwinter. His boat was *Les Quatre Ventres*, a 31-foot sloop. He too overturned in the Le Maire Strait off Staten Island, but he had foreseen the possibility and fitted buoyancy tanks which righted her, and as luck happened she came up with her mast still where it belonged. More recently, the 42-foot ketch *Tsu Hang* with three people on board — Miles and Beryl Smeeton, who owned her, and John Guzzell — driving toward the Horn from New Zealand was capsized lengthwise by an enormous sea coming up astern. They managed to get her into a port in Chile for repairs and tried again next year. But incredibly the same thing happened again, and this time she was well and truly smashed up — mainmast carried away, mizzen broken off short, and the main hatch stove-in — 700 miles northwest of the Horn. Yet, and this must be significant, they survived. Another to be turned right over by a big sea in the Forties was Bill Nance in *Cardinal Virtue*, a boat only 25 feet long. Edward Alcard in the *Sea Wanderer*, who spent a long time cruising in the neighborhood of Tierra del Fuego, was more fortunate, though he too had a rough time in the Le Maire Strait.

Each of these characters had some more or less valid reason for going around the Horn or being in its vicinity; they claimed to be testing, proving, or investigating something or other, or maybe attempting to break some ultimately meaningless record dreamed up to sell newspapers. They fooled nobody who ever thrilled to the lift and swing of a deck underfoot; and the simple fact is that, like Gerbault, they had surrendered to the lure of the sea and become addicted to deep water. Bernard Moitessier not only admits it but glories in it.

Moitessier was born in Indochina of French parents and the first seagoing craft he owned was a junk. He piled her up in the Antilles and landed in Trinidad with 60 dollars to his name and nothing else in the wide world except the pants and shirt he wore. He was then thirty-three years old and, after some heart-searching, he worked his passage to Europe as a deckhand in a Norwegian tanker. Paris was his goal but once he arrived there, he felt shut out, and forever alien:

> . . . like a lost dog without a master in this immense desert of a capital. I had always thought I was solitary by nature, because I could not imagine going to sea any other way than alone. I realised now that solitude at sea was steeped in rich colours, sometimes violent, but always warm, which had nothing in common with this greyness, this total emptiness a man feels without a friend, lost in an indifferent and perpetually hurrying crowd . . .

He had a picture in his mind of the boat that would give him freedom and set about acquiring the money with which to build her. By the time he had raised enough, he had also got himself a wife and a family of children, but the dream remained as bright as ever and his purpose as sharply insistent. He built his boat of steel, welded throughout, and called her *Joshua* in memory of Captain Slocum. Then, having credited her with a soul and the ability to respond in kind to his emotions, he set sail for the Marquesas accompanied by his wife and a little dog called Youki. The children were left at home in boarding schools.

Bernard Moitessier really loved that boat and being in her. She had him for keeps from the very first moment he put to sea in her — the moment he described as "sweet and at the same time terrible." You had to be silent to hear her speak, he said, and:

> . . . You have to be able to listen to the silence, the apparent silence as the wind glides through the sails, the murmur of the water running along the hull and leaving a turbulence behind the rudder, this silence filled with all the small, scarcely audible sounds emitted by a boat that is coming to life. All this you can only appreciate in solitude, or in the company of one who knows how to listen to silence and comprehend the meaning in it. It is only the real seaman who can make himself part of the wonderful state of equilibrium which surrounds him and understand bit by bit, the meaning of the long conversations between the hull and the sea, the sails and the wind.

In spite of his great love of solitude, Moitessier had friends with whom he foregathered from time to time. They were like himself — gypsies who wandered the seas and stayed put only when it was necessary to earn some money to enable them to continue wandering. On this voyage he met a bunch of them in Las Palmas. They included ". . . Englishmen, Americans, two

Germans, a Dutchman, a Norwegian, an Australian, two Frenchmen . . ." Some of these he identifies, rather significantly spelling out the name of the boat first. Among them were:

BOAT	OWNER
Néo Vent	Pierre Aubaoiroux
Aigle de Mer	René Blondeau
Chimère	Bluche
Aventure	Alain Hervé
Vencia	Pierre and Cathy Deshumeurs
Pheb	Henry and Ann Wakelam

The last one was a 55-foot ketch and, like his own *Joshua*, new.

There is no doubt whatsoever about their complete fulfillment and happiness.

> At last [writes Moitessier], we were living, to the full, unhampered by that feeling that we had no time for anything except eternally running to catch the last bus by the skin of our teeth . . . All that had changed; there was no longer a last bus, it was no longer time that dictated but we alone who made the decisions . . .

Moitessier and his wife sailed at last, heading for the Caribbean and Panama, and time became less meaningful than ever. He felt they were poised between sea and sky and though nothing ever happened, they were living as they had not lived for a long, long time. ". . . living with the same intensity as a mussel anchored to its rock," a cryptic statement that he refuses to explain, partly because it would take too long, but mainly because he can't see why we should have to explain everything we do or say.

They continued to sail to the westward, however, and in due course passed through the Panama Canal and set course for the Galápagos Islands, which he calls *the bewitched archipelago* and "a world which Fear has spared." Many have gone there who have found life in big cities intolerable or have simply been unable to come to terms with modern society or subscribe to its values.

Moitessier's intention was to sail around the world, and he was committed to return to France by the following spring because of the children; but the Galapagos put a spell upon him and he overstayed his time there. He went on to the Marquesas and leaving there, instead of continuing to the westward, he headed south and east for the Horn.

It was a wonderful journey he made — 14,216 miles in 126 days — and long before it ended, he was well and truly part of *Joshua* and she of him. He wanted to do "nothing, absolutely nothing, except live in communion with our boat . . ." and his favorite place for doing so was right up in her bow where, he says,

> I spent long moments in a state of semi-hypnosis. It was here that I could really feel the sheer power of *Joshua*, this harmony of strength and

gentleness which emanated from the bow and enveloped the whole boat like a halo. A halo of seven colours . . . including red . . . It was here that I could best hear, with all the fibres of my being the song which the bow had been singing ever since Martinique . . . *give me wind . . . I shall give you miles . . . thousands of miles.*

Joshua got the wind all right. Leaving the Island of Moorea on November 23, 1965, she covered 669 miles in the first week and 726 miles in the second, which was good going but nothing spectacular for a boat of her kind. The fun began when he got into the Roaring Forties, which was around about December 14. That day the weather changed dramatically, with the wind increasing to a whole gale and the sea running wild. Acting on advice he had received in the Marquesas, Moitessier stripped her down to bare poles, disconnected the automatic steering gear and streamed a drogue or sea anchor to hold her head up to the wind, the danger being that if he ran before it she might well broach to or be thrown end over end. The drogue consisted of:

22 fathoms of 4½-inch hemp rope weighed down
    by three pigs of iron of about 40 lbs. each
16 fathoms of 3-inch hemp rope weighed down by
    two pigs of iron of about 40 lbs. each
27 fathoms of 1¾-inch nylon rope weighed down
    by two pigs of iron of about 40 lbs. each

> 32 fathoms of 1¾-inch nylon rope towing the large cargo net as a sea anchor
> 55 fathoms of 1¾-inch nylon rope trailing freely with nothing attached to it

That should have been enough to hold down two boats of her size, but she didn't like it at all and became more and more difficult to manage. She was continually swept by breaking seas and yawed so much she finished up on her beam-ends. He got her up again, but the weather was still worsening, and presently she heeled over and buried more than half her length, her stern lifting in spite of all the weight dragging under it, till the deck stood at an angle of 30 degrees.

At first Moitessier thought the fault was in the boat — that she just wasn't up to that kind of sea — but then he remembered that Vito Dumas had made this passage in a craft half the size and much less well equipped to survive. Digging out Jean Merrien's account of that voyage, he read:

> Whenever the wind strengthened he [i.e., Dumas] left all his sail up and had the boat what one might call planing on the waves at a speed exceeding fifteen knots for short moments. To start with, he says, it is an impressive experience, but one gets used to it. With the boat moving at the same speed as the wave, the wave is no longer dangerous . . .

Moitessier got the message and, cutting all the dragging lines adrift, developed the technique of planing:

> You see . . . the wave is coming up and we are dead before, going at full speed. You alter course the moment the wave meets the stern, the rudder bites well then, the boat suddenly heels and shoots forwards and sideways. Then you bring her back on course as soon as the stern settles down again . . .

The trick in fact is making the boat ride the sea like a surfboard, and he describes the process as being like "driving a 15 ton lorry without brakes down a winding road at 60 mph." And this in 45 degrees south latitude.

> It is impossible to tell the rest of the story [says Moitessier], except perhaps by the fire among close friends when the right words come easily . . . beyond a certain point there is nothing to understand . . . *Joshua* was quite safe, taking the waves at an angle of 15 to 20 degrees. The sea had become colossal and supernatural, and the breakers often covered her to above the dome . . . for six days a man, a woman and a boat were welded together, totally, absolutely in and against colossal seas which they at once hated and loved with all their might.

One month out they had covered 3097 miles, averaging 103 miles a day, and on Christmas Day they were still 2200 miles from Cape Horn. On December 29 their noon position was latitude 43°43′ south, longitude 105° 35′ west, and the day's run 183 miles, the best since leaving Moorea. The ninth of January found them 300 miles west of Cape Horn. This was the height of the southern summer and there was now no real night despite the overcast skies, just "a kind of transition from dusk to dawn." For the 24 hours up to noon on the tenth, *Joshua* made good 153 miles and that evening around 7:00 P.M. she sighted Diego Ramírez, having covered the last 100 miles at between 9 and 10 knots.

The rest was easy. *Joshua* crossed the equator on February 20, ninety-one days out from Moorea, and on March 24 raised Cape Spartel guarding the entrance to the Mediterranean. The destination was Marseille, but foul weather was reported in the Gulf of Lyons and suddenly Moitessier decided he had pushed his luck far enough. Putting in at Alicante, he called it a day. *Joshua* had then been at sea 126 days between ports and had covered, as noted, 14,216 miles. Moitessier himself was wonderfully well and had lost no more than four pounds on the way.

The Horn is no longer what it was. Between them radio and radar have gone a long way toward disarming it. Moreover the area is very efficiently patrolled by the ships of the Chilean navy, and there is usually a British warship or at least a fleet auxiliary around as well. So unless he is able somehow to dodge the newshawks, the loner of today finds himself very closely shadowed and shepherded around the famous cape. But technology has not yet come up with an answer to the westerlies; and the true seafarer like Moitessier hopes it never will, that the Roaring Forties will continue to be one empty place into which he can disappear in search of himself and real freedom.

V

The Blizzard Beaters

THE BIGGEST EMPTY PLACE on the face of the earth and the most inhospitable, the toughest to be in, is Antarctica — the continent at the bottom of the world with the South Pole in the middle of it. It is also, at least up till now, the most useless, although it might yet prove to be a vast storehouse of all kinds of minerals from the basest to the most precious.

The area of the circumpolar continent is approximately 5 ½ million square miles, which makes it bigger than Australia (2,947,581 sq. m.) and Europe (3,800,-000 sq. m.) and slightly more than half the size of Africa (11,500,000 sq. m.). The continent is covered by an enormously thick sheet of permanent ice, from which the huge tabular icebergs — like that encountered by Dana in the *Alert* — calve and drift away to the northward. In the winter the sea all around is frozen to a depth of many feet and the land is unapproachable by ship.

In spite of the enormous thickness of the ice cap, bare rock in the shape of mountain ridges and isolated peaks is found in places, but only at a considerable height. The peaks are called *nunataks*, and some of them go up to 14,000 feet, while the Polar Plateau itself lies 10,500 feet above sea level.

The only plant life is in the form of lichens; but penguins and sea otters in large numbers live along the frozen shores, and places like the Ross and Weddell seas are favored haunts of the whales and those who are hunting them to extinction. Apart from the South Pole, the most important geographical feature of Antarctica is the South Magnetic Pole, which was first located by Sir Douglas Mawson in 1911, 7000 feet up on the ice cap at 72°25′ south, 155°16′ west. The rest is a howling wilderness, implacably hostile to man. Yet it pulls men to it, irresistibly, and those who have been there and suffered its torments are inclined to look back on the experience with a starry-eyed wonder and more than a hint of nostalgia. Thus C. T. Madigan, a member of the Australasian Antarctica Expedition of 1911–1914, could write in retrospect:

> . . . I stood . . . at Christmas time in 1912, on the bay ice on the coast of King George V Land, 250 miles from winter quarters in Adélie Land, and thirty miles from open water, and saw before me, rising from the level white plain of frozen sea, the vertical, red and colossal pipes of a gigantic organ, extending for miles along the coast,

its hexagonal columns of dolerite stretching sky-
wards unbroken for a thousand feet and capped
by the white line of the edge of the mighty ice-
sheet extending backwards a thousand miles to
the Pole. Here was a vast cathedral of Nature,
never before entered by man; only three pairs
of human eyes, one since closed for ever, have
viewed that scene. Remote and still and frozen
as it has been for thousands of years, it lies in
silent, lonely majesty, perhaps never to be seen
again. Whalers cannot get into it and there
seems no reason for a land party to attempt to
reach it for a second time . . .

Douglas Mawson himself had his first taste of it with
Shackleton's expedition in 1907–1909 and confesses that
for many months after his safe return, the last thing in
the world he wanted to do was to go back to Antarctica.
Life was too sweet, civilization too cozy, the society of
ordinary people too pleasant for him ever to opt out
again. But presently ". . . old emotions awakened, the
grand sweet days returned to irresistible glamour . . ."
The voice of the wilderness, the "vast and Godlike
spaces" began to call him and before he knew what was
happening he was hankering for "the stark and sullen
solitudes that sentinel the Pole."

Mawson and Madigan, of course, were only two
among many; but not all that many, for the history of
exploration in Antarctica goes no further back than the
nineteenth century, although in a negative way it begins when James Cook's voyages of 1772–1775 finally

exploded the myth of the Great Southland. The next significant dates are 1839–1843, when a British naval expedition in H.M.S. *Erebus* and H.M.S. *Terror* discovered and explored Victoria Land. Then in 1840, the Frenchman Dumont d'Urville, groping south, reached another point, which he named Terre Adélie. Nothing much happened after that until 1893, when a character called Evensen in the *Hertha* got down to 69°10′ south in 76°12′ west and sighted Alexander Land. A year later the Norwegian Christensen landed at Cape Adare and became the first man to set foot on the Antarctic Continent. In 1900 Carsten Borchgrevink, who had sailed with Christensen in the *Antarctic* as an ordinary seaman, went south again in command of the *Southern Cross*, and landing at the base of Mount Melbourne got to 78°50′ south with dogs. Then came the *Discovery* expedition of 1901–1904 led by Robert Falcon Scott, which discovered and named King Edward VII Land and did a great deal of scientific investigation. The South Pole, however, was the main objective and going toward it Scott got to 77°39′ south in longitude 146 degrees east at an altitude of 9000 feet before being forced to retreat. The existence of a land mass in the Antarctic was beginning to be questioned, but now an expedition led by Drygalski proved conclusively that there was an Antarctic Continent, while Nordenskjold filled in some more of the blank spaces on the map, particularly in the region of Graham Land.

This was the period when Antarctic whaling began to get going, and both the Weddell and Ross seas became populous with improvised factory ships and catchers; but for those with whom money didn't count, the South Pole was still the lure. In 1908–1909 Sir Ernest Shackleton, who had served as a junior officer on Scott's expedition, himself commanded an attempt on the Pole, which sailed from New Zealand in the *Nimrod*. After establishing his base near the foot of Mount Erebus, he started out over the ice with sledges, on October 20, 1908. There were three others in the party — Lieutenant Adams, Doctor E. Marshall, and Frank Wild — and they carried provisions for 91 days. On January 9, 1909, the four men had reached 88°23′ south in 162 degrees west and were 11,000 feet up on a glacier-capped plateau. That was within 100 miles of the South Pole, and it must have cost them an enormous effort to accept defeat and turn back at that point. On this expedition, Shackleton and his companions explored some 2000 miles of the Great Ice Barrier and added enormously to what was known about Antarctica.

In 1910, Captain Scott again sailed for Antarctica, this time in the *Terra Nova*. The expedition was Scott's own, undertaken on his own initiative and responsibility. He obtained grants from various Commonwealth governments, and the Admiralty gave the personnel he selected leaves of absence; but the bulk of the finance had to come from public subscriptions, and the burden of raising it lay on Scott himself. In any event there was never really enough, and it was about then that the element of competition crept into the history of Antarctic exploration; people started waving flags along the Great Ice Barrier, and something was gone forever from the great adventure. The Norwegian Roald Amundsen, forestalled at the North Pole by Robert Edwin Peary, headed south in the *Fram* with the idea of making a dash for the South Pole. Scott had wind of Amundsen's intention before he left Australia and:

> A new element of strain was added to his task of leadership . . . Even now in Australia he was under the galling necessity of breaking away from his proper task to set out from Melbourne "on yet another begging campaign."

Sailing from Lyttleton in New Zealand toward the end of November, 1910, the expedition had established winter quarters in McMurdo Sound and begun its preliminary work by January 12, 1911. Scott was relying on ponies backed by motorized transport for the early stages of the journey to the Pole. He also had some dogs but seems to have had little faith in them for the job in hand. "Their unhappiness affected him powerfully," says Gwynn, and he quotes from Scott's diary to prove it:

> A dog must be either eating, asleep or *interested* [wrote Scott]. His eagerness to snatch at interest, to chain his attention to something, is pathetic. The monotony of marching kills him. This is the fearfullest difficulty for the dog driver on a snow plain without leading marks or

objects in sight. The dog is almost human in its demand for living interest, yet fatally less than human in its inability to foresee. The dog lives for the day, the hour, even the moment. The human being can live and support discomfort for a future.

Amundsen, knowing dogs and how they should be handled, was pinning his hopes on them. He established his base in the Bay of Whales, and the news that he had done so was, according to Cherry-Garrard, fiercely resented by the British Expedition. The implication was that the Norwegian had pulled a fast one on them and Scott himself wrote:

> There is no doubt that Amundsen's plan is a very serious menace to ours. He has a shorter distance to the Pole by 60 miles — I never thought he could have got so many dogs safely to the ice. His plan for running them seems excellent. But above and beyond all he can start his journey early in the season — an impossible condition with ponies.

Knowing the outcome, it is difficult not to find in Scott's writings of this time a foreboding of failure, even a sense of doom, especially when things began to go wrong with the ponies. The timetable had to be set back and it became clear that some of the personnel would have to spend another winter at McMurdo Sound. This created financial problems only partly solved by an agreement to forego payment for the extra season. "Most of us signed the document," says Lieutenant Evans, "but not all could afford to do so." Then, just before setting out, Scott wrote:

> I don't know what to think of Amundsen's chances. If he gets to the pole it must be before we do, as he is bound to travel fast with dogs, and pretty certain to start early. On this account I decided at a very early date to act exactly as I should have done had he not existed. Any attempt to race must have wrecked my plan, beside which it doesn't appear the sort of thing one is out for . . . In any case you can rely on my not doing or saying anything foolish, only I am afraid you must be prepared for the chance of finding our venture much belittled . . .

The expedition started on November 1, 1911 — motors, ponies, dogs, and men. The route they planned to follow took them first across the long snow plain of the Ice Barrier, then up the Beardmore Glacier on rock and ice, and finally over the "interminable summit plateau, a featureless waste of dry gritty sand-like snow." The motors lasted 60 miles, then broke down and were abandoned, the loads they were pulling being man-hauled from then on by Lieutenant Evans and his party. It was 332 miles to the foot of the glacier and the distance was covered at an average rate of 15 miles a day. It was tough going for the men, but worse for the ponies, and three of them had to be shot on the way. Then on December 5 the party was pinned down by a blizzard which lasted four days, and Gwynn feels that "this gravely affected Scott's time-table." The glacier was reached on the tenth and that day the rest of the ponies were killed, the carcases being cached for food. On the eleventh the dogs were sent back and the expedition, reduced to twelve men hauling three sledges, pushed on. The weight of each sledge to begin with was 800 pounds. It was a reducing load, but even so on December 20 they were still hauling 160 pounds a man and that day covered 23 miles. Altogether they marched 126 miles on the Beardmore Glacier, and after establishing the Upper Glacier Depot, they sent back one of the supporting parties. The distance to the Pole was now 337 miles and they pushed on steadily, averaging about 2 miles per hour and 15 miles a day. Then on January 4 the second supporting party started back, leaving five men — Scott, Wilson, Oates, Bowers, and P. O. Evans — to make the final dash. The last depot on the plateau was established on January 15, only 27 miles from the Pole. Scott still had Amundsen on his mind, and in his diary for that day, he wrote: ". . . the only appalling possibility [is] the sight of the Norwegian flag forestalling ours."

Sure enough, next day they encountered tracks of dogs and men which were identified by a Norwegian flag. They went on and reached the Pole on Wednesday, January 17, to find that Amundsen had been there on December 14, just over a month before. Of the place and the moment Scott wrote: ". . . there is very little

that is different from the awful monotony of past days.
Great God! this is an awful place and terrible enough
for us to have laboured to it without the reward of priority."

They spent a day making observations and building
a cairn on which to "put up our poor slighted Union
Jack," then turned for home.

> Well [says the diary], we have turned our back
> now on the goal of our ambition and must face
> our 800 miles of solid dragging — and good-bye
> to most of the day-dreams!

That was on January 19 and four days later they were
showing the first signs of physical deterioration, Oates
and Evans in particular, being more susceptible to frostbite than was normal. On February 4 Evans fell and
suffered a serious concussion, but they got off the plateau onto the glacier and there, among the crevasses that
threatened minute by minute to engulf them forever,
Evans died.

As if that had been the price demanded by the glacier
for their passage of it, they reached the Lower Glacier
Depot without further mishap and started off across the
Barrier with 420 miles to go. On March 2 they came
to the Middle Barrier Depot and found that, though
there was ample food for their needs, the paraffin left
there had leaked away, leaving them without fuel for
warmth and cooking. The next supply was 71 miles

away, the temperature was 40 degrees below zero, they
were down to ten miles a day because of the bad surface,
and Oates's feet were very badly frostbitten.

> God help us! [wrote Scott]. We can't keep up
> this pulling that is certain. Amongst ourselves we
> are unendingly cheerful but what each man feels
> in his heart I can only guess. Putting on foot-
> gear in the morning is getting slower and slower,
> therefore every day more dangerous.

Ten more days they struggled on with Oates not only
unable to pull but delaying them for hours each day
while he struggled into his marching gear. In *The
Worst Journey in the World*, Cherry-Garrard wrote:

> Practically any man who undertakes big polar
> journeys must face the possibility of having to
> commit suicide to save his companions, and the
> difficulty of this must not be overrated, for it is in
> some ways more desirable to die than to live, if
> things are bad enough . . .

Oates was facing that possibility now, and on March
17 he walked out of the tent into the blizzard to die and
become a folk hero, alongside Lawrence of Arabia, Chi-
nese Gordon, and all the rest. But it didn't make much
difference to the others, for on the nineteenth with only
11 miles to go to One Ton Camp and safety, they were
immobilized by another blizzard, of which they never
saw the end. Scott's last words, written on March 29,

were: "For God's sake look after our people," and each reader must make of them what he will.

Two of the men with Scott — Bowers and Wilson — had almost died some months earlier when, along with Apsley Cherry-Garrard, they went on the craziest bird's-nesting expedition that ever was or ever will be. The bird they were after was the emperor penguin, which some scientists believed might provide in its embryo the missing link between birds and reptiles. The only known rookery of emperor penguins was on the sea ice at the edge of the Barrier near Cape Crozier. Chicks had been found in September but it was the eggs that were needed and they were laid in the beginning of July, which is of course in the depth of the Antarctic winter.

The distance from Cape Evans to Cape Crozier is only 67 miles, but in everything except duration, the journey was more arduous and more hazardous than the march to the Pole. It was made in the total darkness of the seemingly endless Antarctic night with temperatures as severe as 79 degrees below zero and over ice the surface of which almost defies description.

> It is at Cape Crozier [wrote Cherry-Garrard] that the Barrier edge, which runs for four hundred miles as an ice-cliff up to 200 feet high, meets the land. The Barrier is moving against this land at a rate which is sometimes not much less than a mile in a year. Perhaps you can imagine the chaos which it piles up: there are pres-

sure ridges compared to which the waves of the sea are like a ploughed field. These are worst at Cape Crozier itself, but they extend all along the southern slopes of Mount Terror, running parallel with the land, and the disturbance which Cape Crozier makes is apparent at Corner Camp some forty miles back on the Barrier in the crevasses we used to find and the occasional ridges we had to cross.

They started out, these three incredibly hopeful seekers, on June 27, dragging two sledges piled high with sleeping bags and camping equipment, six weeks' provisions, and all the necessary apparatus and materials for pickling the penguins when they were found. Cherry-Garrard confesses to "feeling a little frightened" at the prospect before them.

The temperature then was minus 47 degrees F. On June 29 it had dropped to minus 56 degrees F; and on June 30 it touched minus 75 degrees F. At noon on July 6, it was minus 77 degrees F. That was their tenth day out and the distance made good on that date was a mere one and a half miles. Fortunately there was a moon at this stage and no wind, which helped a lot. But on the ninth they were enveloped in dense fog out of which came snow to add to the difficulties. They pushed on regardless and soon found themselves among crevasses.

Even under the ideal conditions of good light, warmth and no wind, crevasses are beastly

[wrote Cherry-Garrard] . . . I dream sometimes now of bad days we had on the Beardmore
and elsewhere, when men were dropping through
to be caught up and hang at the full length of
the harness and toggles many times in an hour
. . . But those days were a Sunday School treat
compared to our days of blind-man's buff with
the Emperor penguins among the crevasses of
Cape Crozier.

From July 10–12, the little party was storm-bound.
In this period the temperature rose over 80 degrees to
plus 9 degrees F and the wind, force 9 on the morning
of the eleventh, reached storm force 10 on the twelfth.
They got going again as soon as the wind eased and:

As we approached Terror Point in the fog we
sensed that we had risen and fallen over several
ridges. Every now and then we felt hard slippery snow under our feet. Every now and then
our feet went through crusts in the surface. And
then quite suddenly, vague, indefinable, mon-
strous, there loomed a something ahead. I remember having a feeling as of ghosts about as we
untoggled our harnesses from the sledge, tied
them together, and thus roped, walked upwards
on that ice. The moon was showing a ghastly
ragged mountainous edge above us in the fog,
and as we rose we found that we were on a pressure ridge. We stopped, looked at one another,
and then *bang* — right under our feet. More
bangs, and creaks and groans; for that ice was

moving and splitting like glass. The cracks went off all round us, and some of them ran along for hundreds of yards. Afterwards we got use to it, but at first the effect was very jumpy . . .

The camping ground they had chosen was 800 feet up on the side of Mount Terror and they arrived there on July 15 — nineteen days out from Cape Evans. As planned they built an igloo of rocks and snow-blocks and after incredible labor and suffering among the pressure ridges and crevasses the rookery was found. Three of the huge birds (they stand 4 feet high and weigh up to 90 pounds) were killed and skinned and five eggs collected. Of their condition when they got back to the igloo that night, Cherry-Garrard wrote:

> . . . this I know; we on this journey were already beginning to think of death as a friend. As we groped our way back that night, sleepless, icy and dog-tired in the dark and the wind and the drift a crevasse seemed almost a friendly gift.

The next day was spent resting and making the igloo more weatherproof. They also set up a kind of stove which they aimed to keep going with blubber from the penguins and, to make more room, they pitched their tent under the lee of the stone and snow hut. In it various gear was stowed, including the cooker, and their finnesko (fur boots). Then they started counting their blessings and somehow persuaded themselves that things could have been a lot worse. This must have been a wonderful exercise in self-deception, for they had already been out twice as long as any previously recorded winter journey, none of which had been made in total darkness and/or such low temperatures or over such terribly difficult going. Consequently, the nearest they had gotten to proper sleep in a month was during the blizzards, when the temperature had risen sufficiently for the warmth of their bodies to melt the ice in their sleeping bags and clothing. The mental strain involved in rising above such conditions day after day was immense and had sapped their strength considerably; and the terrifying journey back across the Barrier was still to be made.

That same night — July 21 — a blizzard swept across the face of Mount Terror. It came out of a dead calm and in ten minutes "it was blowing as though the world was having a fit of hysterics. The earth was torn in pieces . . ." And what was worse, first the tent, then the roof of the igloo were blown away. They were left exposed to the elements with everything gone except what they wore. It looked very much like the end and, curiously, none of them feared it; but there were regrets:

Face to face with death . . . [says Cherry-Garrard], I had no wish to review the evils of my past. But the past did seem to have been a bit wasted. The road to Hell may be paved with good intentions; the road to Heaven is paved

with lost opportunities. I wanted those years over
again. What fun I would have with them; what
glorious fun! . . . And I wanted peaches
and syrup — badly . . . Yes — especially the
syrup . . .

The blizzard lasted three days and for two and a half
of them they were without food. Then they raked together a meal of sorts out of the scattered wreckage of
the camp and miraculously found the tent caught on
some rocks but intact half a mile away.

They started back across the Barrier as soon as the
wind had eased and, wise now, Bowers tied himself to
the tent when they camped just to make sure of it. The
temperature, which had been about minus 21 degrees F
on Mount Terror, dropped first to minus 45 degrees F,
then as low as minus 66 degrees F, but there was a certain amount of light around noon now, although the sun
was not due to lift above the horizon for another month.
This helped; but even so, progress was painful and slow,
seven and a half miles being the best day's march. The
bird's-nesters, however, had become indomitable; they
had gone beyond suffering and beyond fear; all that was
left in them was the urge to get back to Cape Evans with
the three emperor penguin eggs that had survived the
smash-up on Mount Terror. That urge transcended
pain and weariness, and on August 1 they made it.

It was around this same time that Sir Douglas Mawson had his second experience of the ultimate loneliness

in the Antarctic. He commanded the Australasian Antarctic Expedition of 1911 to Adélie Land. This is the French sector of Antarctica. It lies between 136 degrees and 142 degrees east longitude and is in about 70 degrees south latitude — say 1200 miles from the Pole. Mawson called it *the home of the blizzard.*

After establishing a base camp and wintering over at Cape Denison, the expedition split up into half a dozen parties, each with its own specific objective. Mawson took charge of the Far Eastern party — the one that had to go farthest and travel fastest — and he had with him Dr. Xaviour Mertz and Lieutenant B. E. S. Ninnis, both of whom were experts in the handling of Greenland dogs.

Starting off on November 9, they were immediately on glacier ice with tough going because of the sastrugi (pressure waves) and crevasses. By December 13 one of their three sledges had been so badly damaged, it was abandoned and the loads rearranged on the other two.

As they started away on December 14, the surface had improved so much it was "both suitable and agreeable for employment of skis" and Mertz, so equipped, set off in the lead, followed by Mawson and Ninnis in that order. The wind was light, from east southeast, and the temperature 21 degrees F. The three men were content, even happy, and under no pressure or stress about anything, and about noon Mawson, having taken an observation with his sextant, sat on his sledge to work it up. When he looked up again, Ninnis and his sledge had vanished. He had gone into a crevasse, the lid of which had borne Mawson's weight distributed on the sledge but had broken under Ninnis's own weight concentrated on his two feet. Mertz, of course, being on skis, had skimmed across it. With Ninnis went a fortnight's supply of food and the dog team.

The crevasse was apparently bottomless and though the men stayed nearby until nine o'clock that evening, no sign or sound of life came from it. They gave up then and turned for home, which was 315 miles to the westward and 2400 feet below them. The irony of the situation was that most of the food and all the indispensable equipment had been stowed on the rear sledge and the best dogs harnessed to it with the idea of reducing the risk of losing them in a crevasse. The whole of the dog food and all but a "bare one-and-a-half weeks' man-food" had gone, as well as the tent with its floor cloth and poles, the spade, ice axe, mugs and spoons, and Mertz's burberry trousers. Fortunately they were able to improvise a tent from the spare tent cover which had been on the first sledge and Mertz had to make do with a pair of thick woolen underpants. There were six dogs left, none of them much good.

That first day a meal of sorts was made by boiling up all the empty food bags into a thin soup; the dogs had to make do with some worn-out fur mitts and finnesko and a few pieces of spare rawhide harness. Then everything not absolutely essential for survival was dumped and they drove on through the night, following their own tracks back.

What followed was a race, not only against time, but

also against the cumulative effects of semistarvation and inadequate shelter. They went like crazy men, Mertz leading the way, the dogs tearing after him, and Mawson hanging desperately on to the sledge.

> It was a wild race as we careered along, the dogs cutting across the crevasses anyhow with the one idea of catching up to the black figure whirling on ahead. We plunged on to the lids of crevasses and thundered across the sunken ways, crashed into hummocks of ice, sidled on the steep grades and frequently enough capsized and rolled over and over, dogs and sledge and myself, for yards at a stretch . . . After all it was only the pace that saved us. Many of these crevasses were dangerous enough in all conscience, but we plunged across with a tense heart and a grim sense of unreality — such was the effect of the day's tragedy upon us . . .

At 2:30 A.M. on December 15 they reached the site of the camp of three days before, having covered 27 miles of the most difficult and dangerous country in 24 hours. There was of course no darkness at that time of the year. Here they found the discarded sledge, out of which Mertz fashioned a tent frame just big enough to take two one-man sleeping bags and, after killing one of the dogs for food, they got going again at 6:00 P.M. Soon after, it began to snow.

This in itself was unimportant, but it had disastrous side effects:

... The horizon faded into invisibility, the snowy sky merging into the snowy landscape to trap us, as it seemed. There were no shadows to create contrasts; it was impossible to distinguish the detail of the surface, even that directly underfoot. So with gaze straining forward for a hint as to direction, we stumbled onwards over unseen sastrugi ...

In twelve hours they covered twenty miles and camped with Mawson painfully snow-blind in one eye. Mertz treated him with zinc sulphate and cocaine at intervals, but neither of them got much sleep and soon they were off again, traveling now through thick, soft snow.

Because of the close proximity of the magnetic pole, the compass was useless, and with the sun invisible through the veil of falling snow, they had to rely for their direction on the trend of the hard, winter sastrugi which they knew ran approximately north and south. Their salvation lay to the west, which meant they had to keep on, up and over, up and over, endlessly, feeling with their feet for the ridges under the level surface of the snow. It was exhausting work and by 2:00 A.M. on the seventeenth, they were done up and camped, though only eleven miles had been covered. They killed another dog at that point, but it was so emaciated it yielded very little in the way of food.

And now the temperature began to drop and the wind to rise. On December 21, with the temperature around 0 degrees F, the wind increased to at least 40 miles per hour, blowing away the soft snow and polishing the sastrugi to a glasslike surface. Because of the difficulty of keeping their feet, they were down to a bare 13 miles that day. On the next it was snowing again and after six miles they had to camp because of the crevasses. There was now only one dog left.

Christmas Day was celebrated with a dog stew and a run of eleven miles, which left 160 miles still to go. On December 28, the last dog was killed, and they did only five miles. On the twenty-ninth it was seven miles, on the thirtieth over more level ground, fifteen miles; but on New Year's Day they were snowbound and Mertz became ill. It was not until January 3 that they got going again, to cover a mere five miles before the weather, worsening, pinned them down. Mertz was by then suffering from dysentery and had his fingers badly frostbitten. On January 7, Mertz began to have fits, becoming delirious in the afternoon, and in the small hours of the morning Mawson found he was dead.

> Outside [he says], "the bowl of chaos was brimming with drift-snow and as I lay in the sleeping bag beside my dead companion, I wondered how, in such conditions, I would manage to break and pitch camp single-handed. There appeared to be little hope of reaching the Hut, still one hundred miles away. It was easy to sleep in the bag, and the weather was cruel outside . . .

He braced himself for the effort and buried Mertz under a pile of snow-blocks next day, but the weather was so bad he was unable to start again until the eleventh. By now his feet were in shocking state, raw and festering, as indeed was his whole body, and he made a bare six and a quarter miles by sledge-meter before he had to camp again. On the twelfth he was camp-bound in a blizzard; on the thirteenth he did six miles, on the fourteenth five miles, and on the fifteenth, when he encountered partly melting snow and it was impossible to pull the sledge, he knocked himself out over a single mile. The sun came out on the sixteenth and to take advantage of a following wind, he rigged an improvised sail on the sledge. It helped but gave him no extra distance because the going over deep, newly fallen snow was so heavy. It was also necessary to make frequent stops to scrape the caked snow off the runners. He was then in an area where "riven ice ridges as much as eighty feet in height passed on either hand," and the surface was badly crevassed under the blanket of snow. Sometimes he went through with a foot or a leg; but his luck held until the sun disappeared in a snow haze and he was once more groping in a snow-blind light. Five miles was his tally that day and his supper at the end of it was a jellylike soup made from dog sinews.

On the eighteenth he broke camp at 8:00 A.M. under an overcast sky and steadily falling snow — the worst possible conditions in which to cross such a dangerously crevassed area — and two miles out, he went through a snow bridge. For a moment, he thought it was the end, and all he felt was great regret that after having stinted himself so painfully, he was dying before he could eat the food he had saved. Then the sledge stuck in the deep snow on the lip of the abyss and held him dangling there at the end of the harness. The crevasse was some six feet wide and the walls of it descended sheer into the blue depths below. Fourteen feet above him he could see the daylight through the gap he had torn in the lid. Instinctively he hauled himself up hand over hand, but as he lay sprawled across the edge of the snow bridge, it broke away under him and he dropped back the full length of the rope.

Lacking the strength to try again, he made up his mind that this was indeed the end for him; and as he saw it there was no need, or any point in going out slowly and miserably at the end of a rope. All that remained was to slip the harness and go plunging down into oblivion, "the peace of the great release." But something in his nature, perversely unyielding and ultimately uncompromising, rejected the easy way. He tried for the top again and this time made it, collapsing when he reached solid ground and lying unconscious for a couple of hours afterward. When he came to, it took three hours to erect the tent, get his gear stowed and the snow out of his clothes; then, from the relative comfort of his sleeping bag, he contemplated the future and asked himself if he really wanted to go on, whether it was not better to enjoy life for a few days where he was, sleeping and eating his fill till the grub gave out and then just not waking up anymore. It was an attractive proposition, but that unforgiving inner self steadily refused it, and came up with the idea of making a short rope ladder. One end of this he would fasten to the bow of the sledge, the other would be carried over his left shoulder and fastened off on the sledge harness. Thereafter if he went into a crevasse and the sledge was not also engulfed, he would be able to scramble out up the ladder, no matter how much he was weakened by starvation.

He pushed on over ice that was all in motion and making loud booming noises, sharp cracks, and muffled growls; he could feel it vibrating under him, but he kept going and finally got off the glacier late on the nineteenth, pitching his tent on "a snowy slope under beetling, crevassed crags which rose sheer from the valley level some five-hundred feet." Ahead of him lay a climb of 3000 feet and in preparation for it, he lightened the sledge by abandoning all the spare clothing and such gear as the finnesko crampons and the Alpine rope. Then he overhauled the sledge and treated the runners to a coat of waterproofing composition to make them glide more freely on moist snow.

The next day was bad, with the sky overcast. There was also quite a bit of wind and a light drift of snow. He hung on, waiting for some improvement, but at 4:00 P.M. in desperation started out, though visibility was down to a few yards. His day's work was two and a half miles.

And so it went on. On the twenty-first he did three miles; on the twenty-second, six miles; but that afternoon in a brief clearing of the weather, he caught sight of the sea at Buchanan Bay. This must have helped him immensely; but, though his feet had improved, he was in a pretty bad way, with his nails festering and his face and body covered with boils. On the twenty-third he did three and a half miles through drifting, swirling snow, and on the twenty-fourth another five and a half; but he was snowed up on the twenty-fifth and had to dig himself out on the twenty-sixth. He was then down to his last four or five pounds of food, and his physical condition was deteriorating rapidly. Nevertheless, he covered nine miles through falling snow that day only to be forced to hole up again on the twenty-seventh because of the blizzard. Next morning he had a long, tough job digging out the buried tent.

> There was no sign of the sledge which with the harness and spars had all to be prospected for and dug out [he wrote]. It appeared that since pitching the tent the whole level of the country had been raised a uniform three feet by a stratum of snow packed so densely that in walking over it but little impression was left.

He was now over the 3000-foot crest of the plateau and when he sighted Madigan Nunatak in the far-off distance, for the first time he allowed himself to think he might have a chance. That day — January 28 — he did eight miles, all of it in the afternoon, and then after making camp took stock. "There now remained," he wrote, "only about twenty small chips of cooked dog meat in addition to half a pound of raisins and a few ounces of chocolate which I had kept carefully guarded for emergencies . . ." It is impossible to imagine what that little bit of saving must have cost him, and the courage of the man, the indomitable spirit that burned within him, takes the breath away.

The weather was bad again the next day, with a strong wind and much drift, but he pushed on for five miles and then by blind chance blundered through the haze right into a cairn of snow blocks, erected by a party out in search of him and his companions. On the top of the mound was a bag of food with a note giving the bearing and distance of the depot called Aladdin's Cave — east 30 degrees south, 23 miles. He had missed the relief column by six hours and a bare five miles.

With the food question thus solved, the specter of death that had stalked at his shoulder for the last six and a half weeks drew back a little; but he still had problems. The going was bad on slippery ice and though he did fourteen miles next day, most of it was on his hands and knees. That night he improvised crampons but was snowbound by a blizzard on January 31 and finally reached Aladdin's Cave at 7:00 P.M. on February 1. He was then only five and a half miles from the base camp. Held up again, a whole week went by before the weather released him; and it was not until February 8 that he walked into the hut to find the *Aurora* had left that morning, and he was stuck there with the relief party of five to endure another Antarctic winter.

Ernest Shackleton was another who knew the irresistible lure of Antarctica. Having shown the way across the Great Ice Barrier to the South Pole, and having gotten to within 100 miles of it as he did in 1908–1909, most men would have been content and left it at that, especially after Scott, treading in his footsteps, had reached the ultimate goal; but not Shackleton. In 1914 he set out on an expedition that planned to cross the Antarctic Continent from Coats Land on the shores of the Weddell Sea to McMurdo Sound, taking in the Pole on the way.

Again he was balked, this time by his ship, the *Endurance*, being crushed in the ice. The party was forced to take a bleak refuge on Elephant Island. From there Shackleton, with five others, sailed a 22-foot open boat to South Georgia for help and made it.

This is one of the most notable open-boat passages in the history of seafaring and a very famous forlorn hope; but, maybe because the First World War had broken out and given people something nearer home to get worked up about, Shackleton never became a folk hero. He never got cured of the Antarctic either. In September 1921, he left London in a ship called the *Quest*, planning to spend three years in the frozen southern wasteland; but he died on the way and was buried in South Georgia.

As for that dream of a transcontinental journey, in 1928 the American Admiral Byrd established a base on the Bay of Whales and flew across; then in 1957–1958 Sir Edmund Hillary, already famous in the conquest of Everest, did it on the ground with mechanized transport. Today, the Americans have a permanent base at the South Pole, supplied and maintained by air; and recently a ship, especially built and equipped for working among ice, took a party of tourists to the edge of the Barrier. So the land of the blizzard, like the deserts and the high places, yields bit by bit, to the seemingly unstoppable advance of technology.

VI

The Circle Makers

For centuries it was thought the earth was flat and people believed anyone sailing too far in one direction must inevitably go over the edge and plunge into some kind of oblivion. Then in 1519, Ferdinand Magellan, a Portuguese with a grudge against his native land and some rather advanced ideas about geography, sailed westward from Spain with a fleet of five ships provided by the forward-looking king of that country. He never came back but one of his ships did, sailing in from the east to blow up the flat-earth theory and prove conclusively we live on some kind of spherical object that can be gotten around.

In the beginning that going around, or circumnavigation, to use the proper term, was an extraordinary feat of courage and faith; it demanded great fortitude and endurance, as well as navigating skill. Those who did it, their treachery, cruelty, and other sins forgotten, were immediately elevated to the rank of folk hero. But in this, as in everything else, the wonder of yesterday became the commonplace of today and by the mid-nineteenth century there was hardly a seafaring man worth the name who hadn't "sailed round the world" at least a dozen times. They did it only a little more comfortably than Magellan; but in our time so many thousands do it every year in the plastic luxury of cruise ships that it is no longer a talking point, let alone a thing to boast about.

So to make the headlines nowadays, the circumnavigator must have a gimmick — he goes it alone like Chichester and Rose, he does it nonstop like Robin Knox-Johnston or Bernard Moitessier, he attempts it in a trimaran like Donald Crowhurst and Tetley, or he goes around *the wrong way* — i.e., west against the prevailing winds — like the current aspirant to folk hero status.

But whether he goes east or west, the circumnavigator, leaving aside the tourist, who invariably uses the Panama Canal anyhow, has a very limited choice of routes. He can, of course, shoot the Straits of Magellan to dodge Cape Horn; and by going through the Straits of Sunda and feeling his way past the Spice Islands, he will avoid Cape Leeuwin and the Great Australian Bight. But he has no option about the Cape of Good Hope. This he must go around, either way, which means that sometime he will find himself in the Roaring Forties. Moreover, unless he emulates Vito Dumas, who kept south of the three capes and went around all the way in the Forties, he will sail through all the weather zones in turn — westerlies, horse latitudes, northeast trades, doldrums, southeast trades, variables, and westerlies again — and somewhere meet every variety of weather known to the meteorologists. The distance he covers will depend mainly on the route, but in any case it will not be less than 20,000 miles, which is the circumference of the magic circle at the equator. Thus Dumas, although he stayed in the high latitudes, covered precisely 20,000, while Knox-Johnston made it 30,123 miles, and old Joshua Slocum, going via the Spice Islands, stretched it out to 46,000.

The time is another variable. It depends mainly on the weather, but also a great deal on the sailing qualities and seaworthiness of the boat, as well as the seamanship of the man who runs her; and there are other factors, not the least of them being the nature of that man and his reasons for making the trip. Dumas took 401 days, including stopovers; Knox-Johnston, driving himself nonstop, was 310; and Slocum, who couldn't care less about records and believed time was for spending and life for living, made his circle in 1140 days — three whole years and two months.

Obviously, storing and fitting out for a voyage as open-ended and unpredictable as this has always been a major problem, requiring much foresight and organization. Curiously, it seems to have been easier in Slocum's day. He did it on a shoestring at any rate and his staple food was salted cod. This he was given by the owners of the wharf alongside which he lay in Gloucester; they also donated a barrel of oil "to calm the waves." He was given other things too by ancient mariners of his acquaintance, fishermen he had sailed with, and old ladies who cherished memories of him in his bright-eyed youth. The gifts included a lantern for the masthead, and a two-burner cabin lamp which could also be used as a cooker and a heater. He also "took in," and presumably paid for himself, a quantity of butter and a barrel of potatoes. Just how hard up he was is shown by his refusal to spend fifteen dollars on having his old chronometer cleaned and rated for the voyage. He left it at home and took with him instead, as his only timepiece, a tin clock that was priced at a dollar and a half, the merchant letting him have it for a dollar because the face was smashed. For the rest of his needs and the replenishment of his food lockers, he was prepared to rely on the communal spirit of all true seafarers and what the sea would throw into his lap. So he ate a lot of flying fish and was given a variety of food and equipment at every port of call: fresh bread, butter, cheese, and plums at Horta in the Azores; fresh vegetables at Gibraltar; spare gear from various shipmasters in Rio de Janeiro; bags of biscuits and venison at Punta Arenas; wild fruit at Juan Fernández; everything imaginable in Australia including a new suit of sails; while at Port Louis, Mauritius, the *Spray* was completely refitted and restored for free.

At the other extreme, Robin Knox-Johnston calculated his requirements for 330 days and shipped everything. Aiming to make his circle nonstop, he had no other option. For food he relied mainly on cans, though he also found such dehydrated stuff as he was given most satisfactory. Altogether he reckons he had "well over 1500 cans" besides bags, packets, and bottles containing such things as sugar (112 lbs.), potatoes (350 lbs.), onions (250 lbs.), pickles, sauces, salad dressing, whiskey, brandy, beer, and cigarettes. He also provided himself with a comprehensive medicine chest, an imposing list of tools and spares, a rifle and ammunition, a spear gun, fishhooks and lines, two cameras with ample film, and a tape recorder. On top of all this he had 100 gallons of diesel fuel (70 in the tanks and 30 in containers), 35 gallons of gasoline, 5 gallons of lubricating oil, 35 gallons of paraffin, and 4 gallons of methylated spirits, various Admiralty manuals used in navigation, and a selection of charts.

Stowing all this aboard a ketch with an overall length of 44 feet, 28 feet on the waterline and 11 feet in the beam, was a major headache. When the stores were all aboard there was barely room to move below decks, and he had to construct a rack inside the roof of the cabin for his charts, and knock up an extra shelf in the w.c. for his books. Knox-Johnston gave the problem top priority and spent the first few days out systematically arranging his supplies and equipment, to give himself the maximum freedom of movement below while ensuring that everything that might be needed in a rush was nearby and the rest accessible without tearing the ketch to pieces to get at it. A professional seaman, he was following standard Merchant Navy routine; but Donald Crowhurst, the amateur, seems never to have gotten down to it and existed in chaos throughout.

The cost of circumnavigating has increased enormously since Slocum's day. As already noted, his *Spray* set him back, apart from his labor, a little more than five hundred dollars, and he left parish-rigged and on a shoestring. Thereafter he lived more or less hand to mouth, with something always turning up just when he needed it most. For instance, there was the tallow he salvaged in the Straits of Magellan; part of it was sold for cash in Punta Arenas and the balance to a German soap-boiler in Samoa. Another source of cash was the lectures he gave en route. The first of these, at George Town, Tasmania, brought him about three pounds, and in South Africa he made enough by this means to see him through the rest of the voyage. He seems to have had only one really sticky time in this respect — when he arrived at Pernambuco flat broke. There a merchant of his acquaintance — Slocum was a man with a seemingly infinite number of acquaintances — who offered him a cargo of gunpowder for Bahia, the freight on which would have been a big help; but he had to refuse it because accepting would have imperiled his yacht status and let him in for much heavier harbor dues wherever he went thereafter. In the end the same merchant set him up with a loan; then in Montevideo a firm of shipping agents, after docking and overhauling the *Spray* without charge, made him a gift of 20 pounds without strings. He was on his beam ends again in Australia, and until the yachting fraternity took him under its wings, he made out by charging sixpence a head to look over the sloop. He also exhibited a pregnant shark at the same rate.

Of course Slocum lived very simply. His diet was salt cod and potatoes with a kind of biscuit he made two or three times a week. The flying fish he picked up out of the lee scuppers on moonlit nights made up for the lack of fresh meat, and he always had plenty of coffee and sugar. For such a shrewd man he had an odd attitude toward money and was contemptuous of those who made it important. In Samoa he met the widow of Robert Louis Stevenson and admired her greatly because in speaking of his voyage, she "did not once ask me what I would make out of it . . ." And he claimed that as he sailed farther and farther from the center of civilization, he heard less and less of "what would and what would not pay."

Today, the amount of money involved in any circumnavigation makes that kind of question inescapable. Knox-Johnston, for instance, had a boat designed for his nonstop voyage; but the lowest quotation he could get for the building of it was 5000 pounds. Lacking this quite considerable sum, he sailed in the *Suhaili*, which he already owned, although the experts considered her most unsuitable for the enterprise. They said she was too small, too slow, and too vulnerable to boarding seas because of her high deckhouse. But given the boat, it still cost something like 1500 pounds to fit out and store her. Donald Crowhurst's venture was even more expensive. His trimaran *Teignmouth Electron*, originally estimated to cost 6000 pounds, cost almost twice that amount by the time she got going.

A man with so much money lying around loose is pretty rare and seldom has tar on his hands or an itching foot. Sailing around the world alone just for the fun of it is the last thing he wants to know about; but the aspiring mariner must find the money somewhere, and at this point he acquires a partner. He might be called a press agent, a publicity man, or a promoter, but whatever the label, his job is first to find financial backing for the enterprise and then to squeeze the maximum profit from it. The moment he enters the scene, the voyager ceases to be a true loner. He is in fact no longer entirely his own man, for he has commitments, interests other than his own to consider and satisfy, and when it comes to the crunch, what the press agent says, goes. It is easy to see this shadowy figure in the background as a cross between Merlin the Magician and Svengali the hypnotist, and there is no doubt about his power in the world today:

> In the last half-century [says Daniel Boorstin in *The Image*], we have misled ourselves, not only about how much novelty the world contains, but about men themselves, and how much greatness can be found among them . . . Two centuries ago when a great man appeared people looked for God's purpose in him; today, we look for his press agent . . .

The agent's first step is to find a sponsor — some person or organization prepared to put up the money in return for the privilege of having his name or that of his product associated with the enterprise. Thus Crowhurst got the financial backing of the town of Teignmouth as the price of calling his trimaran *Teignmouth Electron*; and afterward the venture was estimated to have brought the place 1,500,000 pounds worth of publicity. But the chief marketable asset of the lone voyager is his story, which a really clever agent can sell over and over again. First he sells off the newspaper rights, then the magazine rights, the hardback book rights, the paperback rights, television and radio rights, foreign language rights, and so on. There are also royalties for the use of the folk hero's name or that of his boat on commercial products and in advertising by the manufacturers of commodities and equipment.

As an indication of the kind of money involved, the *Sunday Times* is reputed to have paid Chichester 2000 pounds for the newspaper rights in half his voyage around the world with an option to renew. Then a press agent, acting for Robin Knox-Johnston, put up the idea of a nonstop circumnavigation to the same newspaper. This resulted in the organization of the Golden Globe Race, with a prize of 5000 pounds for the fastest time around by a single-handed mariner. With his client's chances of winning as the selling point, the agent then got him contracts with both English and American publishers for book rights, with *True*, an American publication, for magazine rights, and with the British *Sunday Mirror* for newspaper rights.

The folk hero status is a trickier subject than the money involved; but there is no evidence that it ever entered into the calculations of any aspiring circle maker, with the possible exception of Donald Crowhurst. There is, instead, every reason to believe it was wished on them by the promoters, aided and abetted by communicators looking for a continuing story that would build up to a dramatic climax and produce a rich crop of banner headlines. Those who succeeded have been burdened with the label ever since, all except Bernard Moitessier who, in no uncertain terms, rejected it and told the wide world and the communicators that he had no interest in their hysterical applause and synthetic adulation.

But leaving aside the ballyhoo, the basic questions remain. In cold reality, how much of an achievement is it for a man to sail alone around the world, and to what extent is he thereby qualified for the folk hero's niche? Motivation is, of course, an important factor and the value of the longest, shortest, biggest, fastest anything dwindles to insignificance when set against Bombard's fantastic voyage, for instance, or Ernest Shackleton's passage from Elephant Island to South Georgia. But any such judgment or comparison is bound to be subjective and conditioned by the values of the society to which the observer belongs. For the rest one can only list the particular hazards.

Of the elemental dangers — high seas, storm-force winds, and poor visibility — encountered by lone sailors, especially in the high latitudes, enough has already been said to show that given a well-built, seaworthy craft, coping with them is largely a matter of steady nerves and self-confidence backed by experience. Other hazards are icebergs, whales, heavy flotsam, gear carrying away, accidents to the person, sickness due to food poisoning or drinking foul water, and falling overboard to be left behind by the boat sailing on faster than a man can swim.

All these are purely physical contingencies and as such can be foreseen and to a large extent guarded against; but there are others, less tangible and ultimately more terrifying and destructive. The first that comes to mind, especially for a man making his circle to break an existing record, is the effect of prolonged spells of head winds and calm. The frustration of such periods is maddening. It can lead to recklessness and even the kind of despair in which the mariner sees himself not merely alone but as one man against the whole world and everything in it.

Then there is the loneliness itself and its side effects. Men alone in empty places are known to have hallucinations. Frank Smythe, climbing within a thousand feet of the summit of Everest, had so strong a feeling of someone walking at his shoulder that, pausing to eat a bar of chocolate, he broke it in two and offered one half to the nonexistent companion. Shackleton had a similar experience on the ice fields of South Georgia after his incredible journey from Elephant Island; and Slocum, ill with a high fever in a wild gale between the

Azores and Gibraltar, thought he had been boarded by "the pilot of the *Pinta*" — one of Christopher Columbus's ships — who took the tiller and brought the *Spray* safely through the storm. Thereafter the presence of this "ghost" was a phenomenon that recurred in moments of extreme stress throughout the voyage. He was almost in sight of home when he encountered the last bad weather — a tornado off Fire Island. "After this storm," he wrote, "I saw the pilot of the *Pinta* no more."

Slocum was a man with a very dry sense of humor and the deadpan manner that usually goes with it; he was also inclined to a very gentle but wry kind of mockery of himself and pretty well everything else. Consequently it is difficult to know how seriously this fantasy of his should be taken. On his longest passage between ports — that seventy-two days from Juan Fernández to Samoa — he claims to have discovered it was not good to be alone:

> So [he wrote], I made companionship with what there was around me, sometimes with the universe and sometimes with my insignificant self . . . I was not distressed in any way during that time. There was no end to companionship. The very coral reefs kept me company or gave me no time to feel lonely . . .

Yet, with Australia behind him, he confesses that on making one landfall he sat on deck and gave way to his emotions. That was almost a year later, on raising Cocos Keeling Islands twenty-three days out from Thursday Island in the Torres Strait.

Another by-product of prolonged loneliness is fear of going mad. Knox-Johnston, described by a psychiatrist as "distressingly normal," was greatly troubled in this way. The difficulty is that a man among other people has a constant check on his thought processes and behavior. If he does or says anything odd, he is immediately made aware of the fact either by the reactions of other people or by comparison with the norm they represent. Alone at sea he has nothing against which to measure himself and might go quietly around the bend without knowing it. There is general agreement that this is what happened to Crowhurst.

Finally, prolonged isolation appears to evoke a powerful desire for recognition. Thus Slocum records having his signals ignored by a steamer in the Atlantic and commented: ". . . it is a prosy life when we have no time to bid one another good morning"; while Knox-Johnston repeatedly denounces the ships that failed to respond to lamp, flare, or flag signals. On one occasion, after all orthodox methods had failed, he tried to alert a ship with rifle fire and failed, though she was no more than 150 yards away. "It was," he declares, "a shattering revelation to me."

Although, as already indicated, motivation — the reason for doing it — is probably the most important factor in a single-handed circumnavigation, it is the craft in which it is attempted that decides whether the exercise is a wonderful experience or a terrifying ordeal and which in the end makes the difference between success and failure. Slocum's *Spray*, for example, was so beautifully balanced he was very seldom pushed. Mostly she sailed herself. Caught in a severe storm on the passage from Samoa to Newcastle, New South Wales, she lay under a goose-winged mainsail with a dry deck while the mail steamer from which she was sighted was being swept and her passengers were knee-deep in water in her public rooms; and on that twenty-three-day passage from Thursday Island, Slocum spent no more than three hours at the helm, including the time it took him to beat up into Keeling Harbour. "I just lashed the helm," he says, "and let her go; whether the wind was abeam or dead aft, it was all the same; she always sailed on her course . . ."

Of course there was never any time factor in Slocum's reckoning. Sir Francis Chichester, however, when he made his circle in 1966, deliberately introduced one. His plan was to follow the route of the nineteenth-century wool clippers and try to match or even better their time for the round voyage. The now famous *Gipsy Moth IV* was specially designed for the job and stood up to it magnificently. She was fifty-three feet long, which is big for one man to handle; but in small craft sailing in heavy seas and long swells, there is a close relation between length and speed; and Chichester wanted speed. He wanted comfort too, but he was prepared to work for both. And he got them. His circle around the three capes was made in just about half the time Vito Dumas took, and when he recrossed his outward track in the South Atlantic to complete the circumnavigation, he had done it almost twice as fast as any other small craft regardless of the size of crew. His longest passage was from Sydney to Plymouth — 15,-500 miles nonstop — and he did the round voyage in nine months. All this, it should be noted, at the age of sixty-five.

The next man around after Chichester was Alec Rose, another enterprising ancient. His boat, *Lively Lady*, was a bit of an antique too. Originally called *Blue Horizon*, she was built of Burma teak in Calcutta in 1948. Her length on the waterline was 31 feet and overall 36 feet, with a maximum beam of 9 feet 2 inches. She was slow, having been built for leisurely cruising, not ocean racing, and the very thought of tackling the Roaring Forties in her would have shaken most men rigid; but not this one, whose outstanding characteristic seems to have been a dogged persistence in the face of adversity and a total inability to give up. What is more, this little greengrocer from Southsea had no sponsor and no commitments to anybody but himself. Nobody and nothing — not even his own conscience — was twisting his arm. He did it just for the ride.

In a world where competition is the most sacred cow of the whole herd, it was only a matter of time before somebody tried to go one better than Sir Francis Chichester by circumnavigating nonstop. The idea seems to have bitten a number of people simultaneously and independently in the winter of 1967. Among them

was Bill King, who at the end of the year began to build
a boat subsequently named *Galway Blazer II*, which
was rigged like a junk and had a hull like a submarine.
He was sponsored by the *Express* newspapers. Another
was Bernard Moitessier, whose *Joshua*, now five years
old, has already been described. Then Robin Knox-
Johnston, a twenty-nine-year-old Merchant Navy officer at home on leave, heard that Eric Tabarly was
building a trimaran, and guessed his purpose was either
to beat Chichester's time for the circumnavigation or
go around nonstop. Immediately the flags started waving. Tabarly, as already recorded, had won the 1964
single-handed transatlantic race and in doing so demonstrated his tenacity, skill, powers of endurance, and
courage. Knox-Johnston writes, in *A World of My
Own*:

> I remembered all the fuss in the French newspa-
> pers when he had won . . . the inference being
> that the Island Race had been proved inferior
> seamen to the French. This had made my blood
> boil at the time and I could picture the headlines
> if Tabarly became the first person to sail right
> round the world non-stop. We'd never hear the
> last of it . . .

From then on Knox-Johnston was hooked on the idea.
Another interested party was John Ridgway, a captain in the Special Air Service who had already made
the headlines by rowing across the Atlantic. His boat
was the thirty-foot sloop *English Rose IV*, and his

best cards were his strength and physical fitness. Chay Blyth, an ex-paratrooper who had accompanied Ridgway on the long row, then acquired a boat called *Dytiscus III* and threw his hat into the ring.

Altogether, by the time the Golden Globe Race got going, there were nine entrants, who started at intervals between June 1 and October 31 as follows:

Ridgway, in *English Rose IV*, a thirty-foot sloop	June 1
Blyth, in *Dytiscus III*	June 8
Knox-Johnston, in *Suhaili*, a thirty-two-foot ketch	June 14
Moitessier, in *Joshua*, a steel-hulled ketch	August 21
Fougeron, in *Captain Browne*	August 21
King, in *Galway Blazer II*, a special junk-rigged craft	August 24
Tetley, in *Victress*, a trimaran	September 16
Carozzo, in *Gancia Americano*, a sixty-six-foot ketch	October 31
Crowhurst, in *Teignmouth Electron*, a trimaran	October 31

The way they fared demonstrates most vividly the toughness of the enterprise:

English Rose IV. After sixty-eight days, Ridgway was forced to retire from the race and put into Recife in Brazil on August 8.

Dytiscus III. After one hundred days, Chay Blyth

was compelled to put into East London in mid-September.

Captain Browne. Fougeron gave up and put into port after being severely battered in the Forties.

Galway Blazer II. Capsized in a storm off the Cape of Good Hope and lost her mast. Put into Cape Town.

Gancia Americano. After lying a week at anchor making final preparations, Carozzo, greatly fancied to win, got no farther than Lisbon on the outward leg.

Victress. After completing the first ever passage of the Horn and the first ever circumnavigation in a multi-hull, Tetley's trimaran broke up with only 1200 miles to go. This was on May 21, 245 days out.

After Nigel Tetley had abandoned his sinking *Victress* for the relative safety of his rubber life raft, there were three men left in the crazy race — Robin Knox-Johnston, who all along had been considered the least likely to survive, let alone win; Bernard Moitessier; and Donald Crowhurst.

It is difficult to write about Crowhurst, the thirty-six-year-old Bridgwater electronics engineer, without seeming to pass judgment on him, and this is the last thing any loner, particularly of the seafaring variety, would want to do. That he was the "fall guy," the victim of the image-makers, is hotly disputed by some people. They say he knew exactly what he was doing and nobody was twisting his arm, which is true enough if his financial problems are ruled out of the reckoning. But he was talking about it for months, even years, before he finally committed himself, and it is a great pity that nobody tried to dissuade him; nobody asked him the right kinds of questions or looked him in the eye and told him to stop kidding himself. Instead he was taken at his own valuation, encouraged in his fantasies, and allowed to talk himself into a situation from which there was only one way out. Tomalin and Hall, after an exhaustive research of the tragedy and a most intimate study of the man, wrote:

> Like many clever but unsophisticated people, Donald Crowhurst was both seduced by the glamour of publicity and scornful of it. He believed newspaper stories, yet thought he could play-act a part in them for an exaggerated fee. With half his mind he thought the magical tales of heroism and scandal were more real than they could ever be; with the other half he thought them such a facile pretence they could be artificially duplicated with little more than good intentions, a bravura manner, and a skilful press agent. And of course, he was bemused by the aura of big men and big money which, to provincial aspirants, always seems to surround all London-based activity. Fame was a game; a bonanza of easy money and flattering headlines which came as an automatic reward for a proclaimed enterprise which — in Crowhurst's mind — was heroic largely because millions of newspaper readers would be cajoled into thinking it so . . .

Having persuaded himself and a lot of other people, at least some of whom should have known better, that he had the Golden Globe in the bag, Crowhurst's first big idea was to borrow or hire *Gipsy Moth IV* for the enterprise. The people responsible for Sir Francis Chichester's now-famous craft, however, refused to consider the proposition, having already decided to enshrine her in concrete at Greenwich as a permanent memorial to the voyage; so the aspiring circle maker decided to build his own, and somehow talked a business associate into putting up the money. The result was *Teignmouth Electron*, a trimaran described as squat and square with a wide sweep of deck over the three hulls on which the only protuberance was the slight bulge of the cabin roof. "If Bill King's boat had looked like a submarine, Crowhurst's looked like a miniature aircraft carrier." She was launched at Brundall in Norfolk on September 23 and from then until she sailed from Teignmouth on October 31 — beating the deadline by mere hours — the story is one of chaos and confusion.

On the eve of his departure things were so terribly disorganized that the B.B.C. man filming the show called off his crew and sent them to buy fundamentals that were still lacking, including flares and even a life jacket.

'Donald had no lunch that day, there wasn't time' [says this commentator]. 'He stood on the boat trying to organise the stuff as it piled on board. Round about teatime we dragged him off

to a local tea shop . . . to have a snack of some
sort. He was in a terrible state, quivering from
lack of sleep and food. There was no doubt he
clearly didn't want to go. He kept murmuring,
"It's no good. It's no good." He knew it could
kill him, but he could never quite bring himself
to say so.'

He did go; and almost immediately the problems he had
ducked or shelved began to catch up with him. Two
weeks out he was ready to call it a day but couldn't face
the consequences of doing so. "If I stop," he wrote in
his logbook on November 15, "I'll disappoint a lot of
people . . . who've supported the scheme, and my
own family . . ." So he argued himself into going on.

He kept going, making intermittent contact with the
world by radio until January 19, when he gave his
position as 100 miles southeast of Gough Island in the
Roaring Forties. After that nothing was heard of him
until April 9, when a message was received by his press
agent saying he was heading up for Diego Ramírez,
from which it was assumed he was in the process of
rounding Cape Horn. Thereafter rather cryptic mes-
sages at intervals described a storming passage northward for home; and these were used by the publicity
boys to whip up excitement about the outcome of the
race. By June 23, Teignmouth was organizing the red
carpet and brass band for the conquering hero while the
B.B.C. made preparations for covering the proceedings
in a big way. The trimaran was sighted on June 25 by

the Norwegian freighter *Cuyahoga* in 30°42′ north, 39°55′ west, the captain reporting that all seemed well aboard her. Then on the twenty-eighth Crowhurst was in touch with Portishead Radio, and that was the last thing heard of him until on July 10, the R.M.S. *Picardy* found his trimaran abandoned in 33°11′ north, 40°28′ west — 1800 miles from home.

The strange craft was hoisted out of the water onto the ship's deck and subsequent examination of the log-books and other documents on board her showed beyond any shadow of doubt that Crowhurst's voyage around the world was a fantasy. It had taken place only in his own mind and neither his boat nor his body had ever left the Atlantic. Through all those weeks of radio silence when he was supposed to be on his way from the Cape of Good Hope past Australia and New Zealand to the Horn, he was wandering between the Falkland Islands and the River Plate, killing time until his phony circle was completed and he could link up fantasy and reality again and head for home.

The last entry in his log was dated July 1, and it is assumed he died that day, getting out of the trap he had talked himself into by walking away from it — over the side; and there is little doubt that by then anxiety about the consequences of his action, on top of the prolonged strain of organizing and maintaining such an elaborate deceit, had driven him out of his mind.

Meanwhile, Robin Knox-Johnston, who was consid-ered the least likely of all the entrants to survive, let alone win, had sailed triumphantly into Falmouth, aboard his ketch *Suhaili*. He arrived on April 22, 1969, and in the 310 days that had elapsed since his departure, he had sailed 30,123 miles at an average speed of 4.02 knots — 96.54 miles a day. The welcome given him exceeded the wildest dreams of the admen for size and mass hysteria.

That leaves one man — Bernard Moitessier — still to account for. For him to have gotten involved in such a jamboree was, to start with, completely out of character. The Golden Globe concept was contrary to all he felt about the sea and ships. Like old Joshua Slocum and Alain Gerbault, he believed life was for living and records were bunk. Nevertheless he was persuaded to let his name be added to the list of entrants, making it quite clear that it wasn't "for the cash nor the glory" — but for the love of life. In his own phrase he went for the good of his soul and wanted no part in any race. He also refused to allow the organizers to provide him with radio equipment, for when he went off on his own, he wanted to do it properly, and once he got going he reveled in the solitude.

> God [he wrote in his log], how good it is to live like an animal, to be caressed by a tepid and soft wind! How good it is to contemplate the Southern Cross, each night a little nearer the horizon. To sleep like a drunkard, to fill your stomach and belch with pleasure, to spread out in the sun

> till you are almost stupefied. I am no longer frightened of meeting men. I am at peace . . .

He loved the silence, the freedom from futile conversations and empty, meaningless gossip, and he felt his whole world change. "What mattered before counts less now, even doesn't count at all. And there are things which were unimportant before which now count a lot." He began to see things "through the skin and the stomach," and he loved the Roaring Forties. He rounded the Horn well in the lead so far as the race was concerned and then, somehow, the news trickled through that he loved the Forties too much to leave them and instead of heading northward for home, he was keeping right on to pass the Cape of Good Hope for the second time.

The consensus of opinion was that after seven months alone, he had gone around the bend, but he denied it. "Don't think I'm crazy," he wrote. "I am in very good health." It was simply that, so far as Europe was concerned, he'd had it.

> I have no desire to return to Europe with all its false Gods [he wrote in his logbook]. It is difficult to defend oneself against them — they eat your liver and suck your marrow and brutalise you in the end . . . To leave Europe and then go back again is senseless, like leaving from nowhere to return to nowhere . . .

If he ever did go back to Europe, he declared, it would be as a tourist, not to live. To his mind the battle that is life was idiotic in modern Europe, and he wanted no more of it.

> Make money, make money — to do what? To change your car when it is still going well, to dress "decently" — this word makes me laugh — to pay an exorbitant rent, to pay for the right to moor one's boat in a port for almost the price of a servant's room in Paris, and perhaps one day to have a television; pushed, forced, ordered about by those false Gods . . . I am going where you can tie up a boat where you want and the sun is free, and so is the air you breathe and the sea where you swim, and you can roast yourself on a coral reef . . .

He went on in the Forties, through the Indian Ocean, across the Australian Bight and the South Pacific almost to Cape Horn again, then turned north and found his sanctuary in Tahiti, which is as near as one can get to the magic spot where nobody asked old Slocum if his voyage was going to pay.

That was the end of the great Golden Globe Race, but the admen and the circle makers are still at it, the latest gimmick being to do it "the wrong way around," in other words, against the prevailing westerly winds, while the drive to *sell* people the idea of "messing around in boats" intensifies. Yachting, screams the commercial, is no longer a rich man's pastime. It belongs to the people and every man with six hundred dollars to put down as a deposit can have his own ocean-going yacht, these days; providing of course that he is prepared to spend the next five years paying off the balance at seventeen dollars per week. So for the true loners the question is, where do they go from here, and it is rapidly becoming an urgent one.

VII

Conclusion

J ET TRANSPORT and rocketry are rapidly changing man's view of the world, but it remains a big place. This brief glance has taken in only the most obvious of the empty places in it and looked at a mere handful of the better-known characters who have haunted them from time to time. A truly exhaustive study, going deeply into the psychology and background of such men, would be a task for the expert, and it is to be hoped that one day somebody will get around to it for the greater understanding of man by men. Meanwhile, a number of fairly obvious points can be made.

The very first thing that emerges about these men whom Kipling has called "the sons of Martha" is the toughness of their chosen line. Whether the urge drives them up a mountain, across the frontiers of knowledge beyond the Great Ice Barrier, over an ocean single-handed or merely into taking a long walk in some howling wilderness, it is no soft option on which they embark, and they know it before they start. Indeed, the deprivation is a very important element in the spin-off, for the pleasure to be gotten from an appetite diminishes the more it is indulged until it changes into revulsion; but there is no end to the satisfaction of denying it. Thus Philby, on his crossing of the Rub' al Khali, after going without coffee for twenty-seven hours, records the fact triumphantly, calling it "a supreme test of Arab virtue"; and drinking at the end of a 55-day stretch without water, he writes:

> . . . never in all my life have I tasted such nectar. Yet it was the water of Naifa, foul, briny stuff with all the properties of the salts called Epsom or something stronger. I had broken my long self-imposed rule of abstinence from water, and I felt amazingly refreshed by the experience.

The important thing is, of course, not that he was thirsty and went without, which is a commonplace experience in the desert, but that wide-eyed, he deliberately elected to do so.

David Pye, writing of Mallory on Everest, puts over the same idea on a higher plane:

> The climbing of the mountain was an inspiration because it signified the transcendence of mind over matter. Nowhere as among the high snow and ice is the utter insignificance of man's bodily presence so overwhelming, nowhere as among

these mighty masses do his desires and aspirations
seem, by comparison, so triumphant . . .

The same is true of the desert wanderer and the single-handed sailor. Each of them has a mystique virtually impossible to communicate to the uninitiated, and the only way to understand a man like Gerbault or Moitessier, for example, is to start sailing the Atlantic alone. Nevertheless it is obvious they work harder for their thrills than anybody ever did for wages; and they toe more lines than the mythical average man in the most tyrannical of communities. The difference is that their lines are self-drawn and the strictness of them proves the folly of calling all dropouts good-for-nothings or equating dissent with anarchy.

Of course the *dolce vita* is well enough in small doses; but the experiences of these men who, for varying periods and different reasons, rejected it, show just how comprehensively and destructively life is cushioned within organized society. By abandoning the benefits and comforts so much taken for granted, they point them up and underline the ultimate effect of too much ease on the human spirit. The common aim of the wanderers is to simplify life again, at least for a while. "Simplicity," says Smythe, "is the soul-mate of happiness," and Gerbault writes enthusiastically of the pleasure to be got just from throwing things away.

> I was in a train de luxe, going towards Madrid
> [he relates in this context], when glancing

through the window, I saw a young beggar. He was running barefoot alongside the train. His brown skin was shining between the rags which covered him. He was more beautiful than the young beggar painted by Murillo, more realistic than the club-footed child of Ribeira. He was begging as they do in Spain, for he seemed to grant a favour instead of asking for one. He was a prince of life, this dirty and ragged beggar, running free in the sunlight . . . I felt I should have liked to have been in his place . . .

This attitude is not masochism and it has nothing whatsoever to do with the peculiar perversion that makes a man beat his head against a wall just to feel good when he stops. There is a genuine gain in the responses as simplification frees them.

I wish [writes Apsley Cherry-Garrard], I could take you on to the Great Ice Barrier some calm evening when the sun is just dipping in the middle of the night and show you the autumn tints on Ross Island. A last look round before turning in, a good day's march behind, enough fat pemmican inside you to make you happy, the homely smell of tobacco from the tent, a pleasant sense of soft fur and the deep sleep to come. And all the softest colours God has made are in the snow; on Erebus to the west, where the wind can scarcely move his cloud of smoke; and on Terror to the east, not so high, and more regular in form. How peaceful and dignified it all is!

Another thing the wanderers have in common is the conflict between the urge to be themselves and the desire to belong to something bigger than they alone can ever be — the contradiction between the pull away into solitude and the gregarious instinct. This is what made landfall such an overwhelming emotional experience for Joshua Slocum. It also accounts for Moitessier's reluctance to leave Las Palmas, his long stopover in the Galápagos, and his sudden decision to end his Cape Horn voyage at Alicante instead of going on to Marseille. And it is at the bottom of the loner's desire to be recognized and acknowledged. Identity is all-important, but in the end it is a function of society and one of the gifts belonging to it bestows.

"No man can draw a free breath who does not share with other men a common and disinterested ideal," wrote Antoine de St. Exupéry in *Wind, Sand and Stars* and, as already noted, what these men were really seeking was not isolation but some simplified form of community within which they could be themselves and do their own things. It was this kind of association that Slocum sensed in Samoa, and Moitessier actually recognized it in the Galápagos:

> In the Galapagos [he wrote], everybody lives on
> his own by himself . . . up on the heights as
> down by the sea there is something that is diffi-
> cult to find elsewhere; a simple life, primitive in
> the noble sense of the word, free from all false
> values. Which does not mean that all true values

> co-exist harmoniously in this extraordinary com-
> munity . . .

But, in spite of his enthusiasm, he was far-sighted enough to realize that the place wasn't for him, and too honest to deceive himself about it. He knew that only a small percentage of those going to this paradise on earth stayed long enough to put down roots, and he bravely set out the reasons. He called them hurdles. The first was the sheer physical hardship — the lack of the cushioning and coddling civilized society provides for its members. The second, curiously enough, was the loneliness — a hunger for a cozier and more total belonging that apparently came on people like a disease after about five years. And then, after ten years, came the problem of the children born in the islands. Would they be able to adapt themselves to life elsewhere if one day they wanted to leave; and had anybody the right to rob them of the choice? Moitessier doesn't say so, but it must have been the thought of his own children, the need to get back to them in France, that finally pulled him away from the Galápagos.

So in the end the loner, even one as unrepentant as Moitessier, comes back, if only for a while; and each time he finds it harder to get away again. The urge is there, stronger than ever, perhaps; but the empty places are becoming fewer and more difficult, more expensive to get at. Technology and the drive of the admen are seeing to that, for as life becomes more complex, more raucous, more of a frenetic rat race, increasing numbers of people are seeking to escape from it, at least for a spell. The exploiters, always on the lookout for the fast buck, have been quick to respond, and the travel agencies are now offering camel trips along the old caravan routes of the Sahara, package safaris into darkest Africa and conducted tours of the Southern Ocean. All this, and the fact that there were forty-three entries for the 1968 solo transatlantic race, is enormously significant for the would-be solitary.

Fortunately for him, however, there is more to a man than his mere physical presence, and the true loner when all else fails will seek the solitude he craves in his mind where neither the admen nor the brainwashers can stop him from being himself alone, even in a crowd, just so long as he keeps on working at it.

*Listed below by chapter
are the sources for quotations throughout the book.*

Introduction

James G. Frazer, *The Golden Bough* (London: Macmillan and Co., 1954).
James M. Scott, *Gino Watkins* (London: Hodder and Stoughton, 1935).
Cecil T. Madigan, *Central Australia* (London: Oxford University Press, 1936).

Chapter 1. Wanderers in the Wastelands

Thomas E. Lawrence, *Seven Pillars of Wisdom* (London: Jonathan Cape, 1935).
Bertram Thomas, *Arabin Felix.* (London: Jonathan Cape, 1932).
Ernest Scott, *Australian Discovery by Land* (London: Dent, 1969).
Madigan, *Central Australia*
Marcel Migeo, *Saint-Exupéry: A Biography* (London: Macdonald and Co., 1961).
Antoine de Saint-Exupéry, *Wind, Sand and Stars* (London: Heinemann, 1939).
Saint-Exupéry, *The Wisdom of the Sands.* (London: Heinemann, 1939).
Saint-Exupéry, *Flight to Arras* (London: Heinemann, 1932).
Harry St. John B. Philby, *The Empty Quarter* (London: Constable, 1933).

Chapter 2. North Atlantic Nomads

Alain Gerbault, *The Flight of the Firecrest* (London: Rupert Hart-Davis, 1955).
Eric Tabarly, *Lonely Victory* (London: Souvenir Press, 1965).
Sir Francis Chichester, *The Lonely Sea and The Sky* (London: Hodder and Stoughton, 1964).

Chapter 3. Climbers on the Roof

David Pye, *George Leigh-Mallory* (London: Oxford University Press, 1927).
J. E. Q. Barford, *Climbing in Britain* (London: Pelican Books, 1946).
Francis S. Smythe, *Adventures of a Mountaineer* (London: Dent, 1940).
Maurice Herzog, *Annapurna* (London: Collins, 1952).
E. F. Norton, *The Fight for Everest* (London: Arnold, 1925).

Chapter 4. The Gypsies of the Horn

Richard Henry Dana, *Two Years Before the Mast* (London: Dent, 1969).
Joshua Slocum, *Sailing Alone Around the World* (London: Rupert Hart-Davis, 1948).
Bernard Moitessier, *Cape Horn: The Logical Route* (London: Adlard Coles Ltd., 1969).

Chapter 5. The Blizzard Beaters

Madigan, *Central Australia.*
Stephen Gwyn, *Captain Scott* (London: Penguin Books, 1939).
Apsley Cherry-Garrard, *The Worst Journey in The World* (London: Chatto and Windus, 1965).
Sir Douglas Mawson, *The Home of the Blizzard* (London: Hodder and Stoughton, 1930).

Chapter 6. The Circle Makers

Nicholas Tomalin and Ron Hall, *The Last Strange Voyage of Donald Crowhurst* (London: Hodder and Stoughton, 1970).
Slocum, *Sailing Alone Around the World.*
Robin Knox-Johnston, *A World of My Own* (London: Cassell, 1969).

Chapter 7. Conclusion

Philby, *The Empty Quarter.*
Pye, *George Leigh-Mallory.*
Gerbault, *The Flight of the Firecrest.*
Cherry-Garrard, *The Worst Journey in the World.*
Saint-Exupéry, *Wind, Sand and Stars.*
Moitessier, *Cape Horn: The Logical Route.*

Other sources used by the author:

British Admiralty, *Manual of Seamanship* (London: Her Majesty's Stationery Office, 1952).
Mildred Cable and F. L. French, *The Gobi Desert* (London: Oxford University Press, 1944).
A. P. Elkin, *The Australian Aborigines* (London: Oxford University Press, 1954).
E. R. G. R. Evans, *South With Scott* (London: Penguin Books, 1921).
Sir Charles Edward Kingsford-Smith, *My Flying Life.*
Rudyard Kipling, *Selected Poems*, Edited by T. S. Eliot (London: Faber and Faber, 1942).
Jean Merrien, *Madmen of the Atlantic* (London: Phoenix House, 1961).
Sir Alec Rose, *My Lively Lady* (London: Harrap, 1968).
Sir Ernest Shackleton, *South* (London: Penguin Books, 1919).
Francis S. Smythe, *Kamet Conquered* (London: Dent, 1932).
Smythe, *Kanchinjunga Adventure* (London: Dent, 1930).